THE FASTEST
WOMAN
ON WHEELS

THE FASTEST WOMAN ON WHEELS

The Life of
Paula Murphy

ERIK ARNESON

FOREWORD BY
"LANDSPEED" LOUISE NOETH

To my mother and first copy editor,
Meredith Arneson.
"Miss you, Mom."

Contents

Foreword
By "LandSpeed" Louise Noeth
ix

Acknowledgments
xiii

Introduction
xv

Chapter 1
How Do You Like Them Apples?!
1

Chapter 2
Origins of Speed
23

Chapter 3
Life's a Drag (1965–1970)
47

Chapter 4

NASCAR Stars and Rocket Cars (1971–1975)

77

Chapter 5

Around the World in a Pontiac Sunbird

107

Chapter 6

Finishing the Ride

127

Bibliography

143

Author Interviews

149

Index

151

About the Author

158

Foreword

By "LandSpeed" Louise Ann Noeth

I met Powerfully Potent Perpetual Paula long after she had retired from making her living in helmets and fireproof underwear.

She granted me an interview about her time on the Bonneville Salt Flats, driving a jet dragster in the early 1960s, and hasn't been able to get me out of her hair ever since. Then, as it is today, her recall was as clear and detailed as if her virginal thrust-powered runs had been made last week, not thirty years ago.

Unlike the "formula" conversational tone rampant in today's on-camera reporting, Paula was at ease, and I marveled at how she recounted milestone race driving events as if they were ticking off items on a grocery list. I discovered a woman possessed of a terrific, astute sense of humor delivered in "just right" amounts at unsuspecting times.

She gave me full and free access to a filing cabinet filled with photos and documentation of her numerous pioneering roles in not only motorsports competition, but precision driving missions that circled the globe.

To this day, I am her most devoted fan and friend, but ever mindful of my journalistic duty to share this lady's accomplishments in a reality-based fashion. For years, I've written about and included her in a variety of articles, determined to keep her name and legacy alive—always hoping a book publisher or film producer might take up the job.

So, when author Erik Arneson first began his research on Paula for this book you hold in your hands, I was instantly "at the ready" to assist. Arneson has delivered to readers a complicated, multifaceted motorsports story written so anyone can enjoy the saga of a woman with exceptional motorsports credentials.

Pick any female name competing today and doubtless you will find their pathway was forged in part by what Paula did upwards of fifty years ago. Arneson knew this going in, and he understood that her story was like a three-foot-long sandwich that was impossible to enjoy unless you cut it up in digestible parts. He has delivered.

This is in-step with Paula's remarkable ability to proficiently drive any vehicle offered to her and Arneson tells all. In her day, Paula beat the pants off competition that was 99 percent male. She endured loads of goofy, sometimes particularly mean, vulgar prejudice for no other reason than she was a woman. Through it all she was always a lady whose conduct both on and off the track is a lesson in elegant diplomacy. Imagine this woman beating the boys at their own game "fair and square"—at speed or with exacting precision—then touching up her lipstick before she collects her trophy. Sweet.

Longtime sponsor, the late Andy Granatelli aptly noted, "She's made a mark that will live in racing history as the greatest of all US girl drivers . . . a credit to our sport. A careful, brave, consistent and thoughtful example to all racers regardless of race, color, creed or sex."

As this is written, Paula is now ninety-five years old and still driving on her own. For much of the world this might sound dangerous and dumb. It pleases me to tell you that once this woman—who daily relies on a rolling walker—straps into her automobile, the corporeal years vaporize, and she is in full control. Her perception is still laser sharp. It is amusing to listen to her grumble aloud about the poor driving habits exhibited by those sharing the roads with her. Ditto for highway speeds. She often sees errors before I do! Had I not experienced it repeatedly, I might not have believed it. Even now, some might think I am making this up. I assure you she is not only capable but would give Mario Andretti cause for pause as she passed him.

Hanging with her is such a joy! I no longer ask—I make her drive—and will do so evermore.

Geez, Louise.

"LandSpeed" Louise Ann Noeth raced jet dragsters, helped capture the current 458-mile-per-hour World Wheel-Driven Record, and guided Craig Breedlove's and Steve Fossett's teams after a career test driving new cars and trucks for magazines and newspapers around the world. Her books, photos, articles, and award-winning Fuel For Thought columns are touchstones throughout land speed racing. Her writing, photography, and public relations efforts have been honored dozens of times with professional accolades throughout a career that is still at full throttle.

Acknowledgments

First, I'd like to sincerely thank Paula and her son, Danny Murphy. I honestly thought I was done writing motorsports biographies after working on very rewarding projects about racing superstars Darrell Gwynn, John Force, and Mickey Thompson. But, after an extended phone conversation with Danny, I accepted the privilege of telling his mother's story. For Danny, it was about nothing but securing Paula's legacy. The conversation was authentic, honest, and inspiring. Thank you, Danny, and to Paula, thank you for your trust.

In starting this project, multiple early voices helped create the excitement and confidence that Paula's story was full of accomplishments, special moments, and lots of surprises along the way—that it was a tale most certainly worth telling.

Thank you to "LandSpeed" Louise Noeth for your passion for Paula and *all* things Bonneville; Patti Williams, Acting Chair, Archives Center at the National Museum of History; Leigh Gialanella, who helped me navigate my first visit to the archives and the Andy Granatelli Collection; and H. A. "Humpy" Wheeler for always being available and willing to add color and context.

As this book project was in the works, a documentary was also in development. *Paula Murphy—Undaunted* was put together by Cindy Sisson and my FOX Sports colleague, Pam Miller.

I appreciated the back-and-forth conversations and sharing of assets between the two projects.

Thank you to friend Ellen Scherner for help with research about the US Bicentennial Global Record Run.

A special thanks to legendary Motorsports Hall of Fame of America racers Don "The Snake" Prudhomme, Shirley Muldowney, "Big Daddy" Don Garlits, "TV Tommy" Ivo, Don Schumacher, Della Woods, and the incomparable "First Lady of Motorsports" Linda Vaughn, for lending your voices and unique perspectives.

After losing my mother, Meredith Arneson, in 2022, my long-time friend and colleague, Megan Englehart, stepped up to be my first line of copy editing on this project. A trusted eye and an honest voice are always a writer's best assets, and she provides both without hesitation.

Thank you also to Octane Press CEO and publisher, Lee Klancher, for the opportunity to tell this story, and my editor, Faith Garcia, for helping to shape the narrative.

And finally, and most importantly, thank you to my wife, Sandy, and my kids, Eileen, Kyle, Jaret, and Dakota, for being my source of inspiration to be better, to do good, and to challenge myself. Thank you and I love you!

Introduction

Lyndon Johnson was president. *Bonanza* was the number one show on television, and the Beatles had just wrapped up their first US tour after famously appearing on the *Ed Sullivan Show* earlier in the year.

As an eventful 1964 neared its close, a little more than an hour from the Nevada-Utah border-straddling town of Wendover, a thirty-six-year-old single mother of one, who grew up modestly in Cleveland, found herself unassumingly on the brink of history as she stared alternately at the vastness of the famed Bonneville Salt Flats and back again at a homemade, jet-powered hot rod she had never laid eyes on before that moment.

"When I got [to Bonneville] and saw the car for the first time, I said to myself, 'Hmmm, do I really want to drive this thing?'" recalled Paula Murphy, now ninety-five and living in California.

Her job appeared simple enough—point it straight and go fast. After all, there was nothing around for miles but salt. However, there were more than a few impediments to completing the high-speed task. The first and most obvious—she didn't fit in the car. The cockpit had been designed and built for a man with larger proportions. But with the aid of a strategically placed pillow or two, Murphy, who had been making her name on the California sports car racing circuit for several years, piloted speed pioneer Walt

Arfons's open-cockpit, jet-powered Avenger across the Bonneville Salt Flats for a two-way average speed of 226.37 miles per hour.

Looking to take advantage of growing national interest in the ongoing automotive speed wars on the salt—and all of the activity in the advertising arena that surrounded it—motorsports mover-and-shaker Andy Granatelli brokered a deal with Arfons via an STP sponsorship. Granatelli enlisted Murphy. Her pay for the effort: ten dollars for every mile per hour, plus expenses. A day later, and more than 2,000 miles away, the *New York Times* ran an easy-to-miss, five-paragraph story in the middle of page forty-two with the two-deck headline:

Land Speed Record
For Women Broken

There were plenty of reasons along the way to back out or say "no, thanks," but Murphy fulfilled her commitment, never outwardly flinching throughout the hastily-thrown-together effort. Fortified by a Midwestern work ethic instilled by her father, Murphy stayed on task.

"That's the only way," Murphy reflected the following year for *Modern Rod* magazine. "If I had time to sit around and think about it, I might have chickened out. Of course, I was scared."

With pre-run instructions that Murphy recalled included little more than, "on the right is the accelerator and on the left is the brake," she climbed in.

Additional explanation, however brief, was given, and simple controls included a brake pedal on the floor and three levers on the left side of the cockpit—the throttle, the afterburner, and the parachute brake. Due at least in part to Murphy's inexperience, the deteriorating Bonneville surface conditions, and, in all honesty, to keep her away from any of the men's speed records, Murphy was instructed not to use the afterburner.

Under less-than-ideal conditions at the famed Bonneville Salt Flats, Paula Murphy became the "World's Fastest Woman on Wheels," piloting Walt Arfons's homemade, jet-powered Avenger to a women's world speed record. *LandSpeed Productions Research Library / Paula Murphy Collection*

"In order for me to reach the brake pedal, they had to stuff a big pillow behind my back, which raised me up in the seat [and above the small visor], and I got the full blast of the wind when I was making the run," Murphy said. "The strain on my neck and the force of the wind was quite a distraction."

According to an April 1965 article in *Floyd Clymer's Auto Topics* magazine, Arfons was confident Avenger was a safe ride for Murphy, who would be piloting a jet-powered car for the first time. Powered by a 2,000-plus-pound Westinghouse J46 jet engine designed for navy airplanes, the hot rod, which looked like little more than a chair in front of a horizontal stack of beer kegs, had made nearly a hundred dragstrip runs over the quarter mile, hitting 200 mph or better on every run—without incident.

Avenger was designed and constructed in Arfons's Akron, Ohio, shop on Pickle Road, in a space he shared with his half-brother and fellow speed chaser, Arthur. Described by *Sports Illustrated* writer Jack Olsen, Arfons's workspace was a "dark place with grimy windows looking into a clutter of jet engines, shelves lined with aircraft instruments and cannibalized parts of old automobiles, airplanes and trucks."

The hot rod on the salt that day was born much like Frankenstein's monster in a garage not unlike many others scattering the American landscape, albeit with the uniqueness of a few jet engines. The other distraction for Murphy—a soaking wet course and continuing precipitation at Bonneville. With a mixture of rain, snow, and hail falling on the course the night before, there was some doubt if the Arfons group would get a chance to make any passes at all.

"The [Avenger] had never been run more than a quarter of a mile. I only had about three miles of usable salt," Murphy said in a July 1970 article in *Hot Rod* magazine.

Distractions and safety concerns aside, and with Granatelli's giant STP stickers slapped to any available space on the car, it was time to get things started. Driver Bobby Tatroe, on-site to both pilot Arfons's Wingfoot Express and act as drag strip pilot for Avenger, gave the hot rod a test run, clearing the way for Murphy's attempt. Murphy continued her preparation, putting her trust in the team, while noting that without jet car experience, it was mostly, "monkey see, monkey do."

"Bobby Tatroe showed me all the things to do, and he set the throttle," Murphy said in *Hot Rod* magazine. "It had a hand throttle and he must have set it at about 80%. You sit there with your foot on the brake while the power builds up, and when a little red light comes on, you're supposed to go. So, when the light came on, off I went. I figured I could just sit inside and go along for the ride. Well, that car was all over the course. Scared me to death."

Murphy's historic effort was recorded in detail in an unattributed feature, most likely with contributions from STP PR, that ran word-for-word in multiple publications, including the February 1965 edition of *Modern Rod* and as an April cover story for *Floyd Clymer's Auto Topics* magazine: "After five minutes of final instructions, Paula took a deep breath and told the USAC man with the walkie-talkie that she wanted to run through the course to the other end. She asked to be timed, but warned it would not be a fast run, 'only practice.'"

The whine of Avenger's jet engine was not unfamiliar to Murphy, having seen similar jet cars run at local drag strips. Being strapped inside one, however, was a little different. After belching out a ten-foot flame, the power in the screaming engine began to build, and according to the article, Murphy released the brake and "disappeared into a haze of salt, dust and spray."

The wet salt struggled to hold the hot rod, with Murphy going into a two-city-block-long fishtail before using the parachutes in an attempt to correct the trajectory. When she finally came to a stop, Avenger was parked in four inches of water and the chutes were soaking wet.

Her proud response, once USAC officials, her crew, and media reached the car: "How'd you like them apples?"

The call from USAC came across the walkie-talkie. Murphy's first-pass speed was 236.00 mph. But to set the record, she'd have to pack up the wet parachute and make the required return pass. Her confidence shaken, but still intact, Murphy replied, "Let's get going back the other way."

Within minutes, the car was checked out and ready to run in the opposite direction across the weather-soaked surface. Running a little less throttle on the return run, Murphy clocked in at 217.50

mph for the second flying mile, giving her a two-way average speed of 226.37 mph.

"I didn't scare myself quite so much that time, but it's still a mighty quick trip," Murphy said in the article. Joe Petrali, chief steward for USAC and FIA, ran up with her averages and asked if she wanted to try another run back to tie up the slow one and thus get a faster two-way average.

A picture-perfect day at the Bonneville Salt Flats hides the fact that the course had been subject to rain, sleet, and snow prior to Paula Murphy's record run—a run that included a parachute maneuver in nearly four inches of water to avoid losing control of Avenger. *LandSpeed Productions Research Library / Paula Murphy Collection*

"I think that's enough for one day . . . I'm satisfied . . . I know I can do it . . . and we do have a new record."

"That's a smart decision," Petrali answered.

Murphy had her record. Granatelli had his publicity.

The Avenger effort, sponsored by Andy Granatelli and STP,
landed Paula Murphy on the world stage, kicking off more
than a decade of high-profile milestones for women in racing.
LandSpeed Productions Research Library / Paula Murphy Collection

Chapter 1

How Do You Like Them Apples?!

"Bonneville has become worse than Darlington or Daytona or any of the major places where the death factor is present. Nothing approaches this place for tension during a week when somebody's going for the land-speed record. It's much more tense than the Indianapolis 500."
—*Humpy Wheeler, 1965* Sports Illustrated

Murphy was no stranger to the otherworldly location ninety minutes west of Salt Lake City, having been to Bonneville in 1963, the year before her jet-powered record attempt, with Andy Granatelli, his brothers Vince and Joe, fellow driver Barb Nieland, and about twenty mechanics for a massive publicity push, highlighted by a collection of record-chasing 1964 production Studebakers, including the Hawk, Lark, and Avanti.

STP was originally an acronym for *Scientifically Treated Petroleum*, but Studebaker changed the STP reference to *Studebaker Tested Products*, naming Granatelli as CEO of the newly acquired business. The Bonneville group collected nearly 350 speed records over a ten-day period, with Joe and Paula setting twenty-one flying-start marks in the Gran Turismo Hawk. Murphy also set the mark for world's fastest woman in a production car on October 17, 1963, topping 160 miles per hour in car No. 9, the 1963 R-3-engined Avanti. The effort was not without a little adventure.

"We were driving the smaller cars on a measured course, but when we started doing the bigger cars in ten-mile circles, I think I got a little overconfident," Murphy recalled. "I slid off the course and across the salt. It was a little like sliding in snow."

Hot Rod Magazine's Bonneville wrap-up, more than a bit condescending in its approach, acknowledged the successful inclusion of Murphy and Nieland: "The girls were well enough schooled to keep the cars going straight on the salt and to keep the engines running sweet and hot. Not a single mechanical failure went into the books during the whole 10 days, and through many of the runs, including one all-girls run going out 1,000 miles, the hood remained sealed during the entire time and only a half pint of oil was consumed."

The effort landed Murphy on the popular CBS nighttime game show, *What's My Line?* in December 1963. Her line: Automobile Test Driver/Set New Women's Speed Record. One of the panelist's questions drew a bit of a chuckle from Murphy and host John Daly: "Does your vehicle fly or stay on the ground?" This was a fair question when it came to running cars across the salt flats.

The feats at Bonneville also cemented a relationship between Murphy and Granatelli, a union that would see the now STP-badged Murphy collect quite a few more "firsts" behind the wheel of a wide variety of automobiles, including Avenger. And for Studebaker, the Bonneville consumer car endeavor was immediately added to dealer tool kits. A note from D. E. Weston Jr., Studebaker's marketing

UNITED STATES AUTO CLUB   CLASS *Jet*
FEDERATION INTERNATIONALE de L'AUTOMOBILE   SPEED TRIALS

F. I. A. Listing
USAC SANCTION NO. *64-5R*
DATE *November 12 1964*
Bonneville Salt Beds-Utah

ORIGINAL~OFFICIAL TIMING MACHINE TAPE OF CONTEST COMMITTEE,
UNITED STATES AUTO CLUB ELECTROMATIC TIMING MACHINE.

(handwritten annotations on timing tape:)
2:49:1 7.59 3
2:49:2 3.65 8
2:49:3 2.8 4 7
November 12-1964
U.S.A.C. Sanction
Number
Car Walt Arfons
Avenger
Driver Paula Murphy
Original Timing
Machine Tape of
the U.S.A.C. Electro-
matic Timer
(Beckman) as
approved by USAC
Records
Flying 1 Mile & 1 kilo
3:09:4 6.60 8
3:09:5 7.09 5
3:10:0 3.16 0
Chief Steward U.S.A.C.
Chief Timer U.S.A.C.
Chief Scorer U.S.A.C.
Run
Notth
Run
South

We hereby certify that the timing machine tape attached hereto is the original and
official tape of the Contest Committee of the United States Auto Club Electromatic
Timing Machine and that the impressions thereon were caused by the passage of the
Walt Arfons Avenger on the record runs certified to in this
report; and we further certify that the timing machine was STARTED and was in
OPERATION from *11:00 AM* **3** hours
prior to start of the official record attempt.

Joe Petrali
Chief Steward, Member Contest Committee
United States Auto Club and
Federation Internationale de L'Automobile

T. Ben Torres
Chief Observer, Contest Committee, United States Auto Club
and Federation Internationale de L' Automobile

John A. Witton
Chief Timer, Contest Committee, United States Auto Club
and Federation Internationale de L' Automobile

SKB Hook
Chief Scorer, Contest Committee, United States Auto Club
and Federation Internationale de L'Automobile

The United States Auto Club timing slip for Paula Murphy's record run behind the wheel of Avenger, a car she had never driven before that day. As the cockpit was not built for her small frame, Murphy needed a pillow behind her back just to be able to reach the controls. *LandSpeed Productions Research Library / Paula Murphy Collection*

manager, found in the Granatelli Collection archives at the Smithsonian, said it all:

To all Studebaker dealers:

The Studebaker's performance team's sensational record-breaking assault on United States Auto Club records at the Bonneville Salt Flats is stirring news to every Studebaker dealer in merchandising the 1964 models.

UNITED STATES AUTO CLUB
FEDERATION INTERNATIONALE de L'AUTOMOBILE

CLASS _Jet_
SPEED TRIALS

Bonneville Salt Beds ~ Utah
Date _November 12 1964_
USAC Sanction No. _64-5R_
F. I. A. Listing

Automobile _Walt Arfons Avenger_   Course _3 Mile Straightaway_   Driver _Paula Murphy_

Distance _Flying 1 Kilo_

North Run	2:05 P.M	Recording	Time	Speed M.P.H.
Finish Time		2-49-32.847		
Start Time		2-49-23.658	9.189"	243.44
South Run	2:25 P.M			
Finish Time		3-09-57.095		
Start Time		3-09-46.608	10.487"	213.31
Time - - Two Directions			9.838"	
Official Average	227.38			

We, the undersigned, served as the regularly appointed officials of the Contest Committee of the United States Auto Club and Federation Internationale de L'Automobile, in connection with the above times and record run of _Paula Murphy_
driving the _Walt Arfons Avenger_
under United States Auto Club Sanction _64-5R_
and we HEREBY CERTIFY that the above times and speeds are correct as shown and were made in accordance with all Rules and Regulations of the United States Auto Club Contest Committee and the Sporting Commission of the Federation Internationale de L'Automobile.

Joe Petrali
Chief Steward, Member Contest Committee
United States Auto Club and
Federation Internationale de L'Automobile

L. T. Ben Torrey
Chief Observer, Contest Committee, United States Auto Club
and Federation Internationale de L'Automobile

John S. Witton
Chief Timer, Contest Committee, United States Auto Club
and Federation Internationale de L'Automobile

J. H. Hook
Chief Scorer, Contest Committee, United States Auto Club
and Federation Internationale de L'Automobile

These News-Bulletins (and those yet to follow) give you the straight, hard facts of Studebaker performance and endurance and point out the tremendous advantage you have over competition.

Place these News-Bulletins on your salesfloor next to the recently mailed posters titled, "It's Official . . ." and "Studebaker Shatters All USAC Records," so every prospect who comes into your dealership is made aware of these Studebaker records . . . and then you will start smashing a lot of sales records.

UNITED STATES AUTO CLUB   CLASS _Jet_
FEDERATION INTERNATIONALE de L'AUTOMOBILE   SPEED TRIALS

Date **Bonneville Salt Beds ~ Utah**
Date **November 12 1964**
USAC Sanction No. **64-SR**
F. I. A. Listing _____

Automobile **Walt Arfons Avenger**   Course **3 Mile Straightaway**   Driver **Paula Murphy**

Distance **Flying 1 Mile**

North Run	**2:05 PM**	Recording	Time	Speed M. P. H.
Finish Time		2-49-32.847		
Start Time		2-49-17.593	15.254"	236.00
South Run	**2:25 PM**			
Finish Time		3-10-03.160		
Start Time		3-09-46.608	16.552"	217.50
Time - - Two Directions			15.903"	
Official Average	**226.37**			

We, the undersigned, served as the regularly appointed officials of the Contest Committee of the United States Auto Club and Federation Internationale de L'Automobile, in connection with the above times and record run of **Paula Murphy** driving the _____ **Walt Arfons Avenger** under United States Auto Club Sanction **64-SR** and we HEREBY CERTIFY that the above times and speeds are correct as shown and were made in accordance with all Rules and Regulations of the United States Auto Club Contest Committee and the Sporting Commission of the Federation Internationale de L'Automobile.

Joe Petrali
Chief Steward, Member Contest Committee
United States Auto Club and
Federation Internationale de L'Automobile

L. T. Ben Torrey
Chief Observer, Contest Committee, United States Auto Club
and Federation Internationale de L'Automobile

John S. Witton
Chief Timer, Contest Committee, United States Auto Club
and Federation Internationale de L'Automobile

H. F. Hook
Chief Scorer, Contest Committee, United States Auto Club
and Federation Internationale de L'Automobile

For external publicity, Granatelli enlisted the assistance of *Los Angeles Times* auto-editor-turned-public-relations-specialist Bill Dredge to spread the word. Dredge's publicity plan included capturing color photography, a push to secure a *Life Magazine* exclusive—with back-up plans to secure coverage by The Associated Press (AP) and United Press International (UPI)—and standard distribution via Studebaker PR to automotive and trade outlets.

UNITED STATES AUTO CLUB
FEDERATION INTERNATIONALE de L'AUTOMOBILE

CLASS _Jet_

SPEED TRIALS

Bonneville Salt Beds

USAC SANCTION No. _64-SR-_   _3_ Mile Straightaway
F.I.A. Listing

I, _Ben Torres_ , and my assistants were observers and were stationed along the entire course and opposite each Lightray, during the record run of the _Walt Arfons Avenger_ driven by _Paula Murphy_ for ~~his~~ her _Flying Mile & Kilo_ records and certify that only the passage of the _Walt Arfons_ car running for this record caused the printing of the times shown on the Timing Tape. I further certify that in establishing the record claimed _Paula Murphy_ drove the car in both directions of the course within an hour.

L. T. Ben Torres

Chief Observer, Contest Committee, United States Auto Club, Federation Internationale de L'Automobile

Through it all, Murphy simply kept driving cars. "I feel I'm doing what not too many women do," Murphy said in the *Akron Beacon Journal*. "It's kind of a pioneer spirit. And I get a thrill from the speed. It's the idea of being in control of this big machine."

The success she was having didn't hurt.

"It's wonderful to be doing something well and winning," she added.

UNITED STATES AUTO CLUB
FEDERATION INTERNATIONALE de L'AUTOMOBILE

ENGINEER'S CERTIFICATE

I hereby certify that on _November 9 1964_ I measured the _1 Mile and 1 Kilo_ distances along the record course at _Bonneville Salt Beds Utah_ and established points for the beginning and end of these distances at _5280 feet and 3280.83 feet_ . I also certify that the gradient of the entire course is less than _one percent_.

SHSHook
Calif R.E. # 1281

Layout of Course
Bonneville Salt Beds ~ Utah
United States Auto Club
Sanction № 64-SR-
November 1964

Earlier in 1964, prior to her success with *Avenger*, Murphy returned to Bonneville with Studebaker to best her own mark with a run of 161.23 mph in an Avanti fitted with the optional Paxton supercharger. And while cars trying to go faster than other cars drew attention around the world, it was the vast setting at Bonneville that provided the elements so totally necessary to great storytelling and active imaginations. Very few people have experienced the Bonneville Salt Flats in person, elevating the feat above others. Reports of Murphy's exploits on the salt may have just as easily been coming from the moon.

"It's kind of like being dropped on another planet," Murphy said. "Miles and miles of white in every direction. It's truly a unique place . . . I'd never want to be out there in the dark."

Jack Olsen nailed it with his 1965 description in *Sports Illustrated*, just months after Murphy's record-setting run: "The mecca of straightaway land speed is 200 square miles of shimmering, crystalline salt as white as fresh snow and as inviting as Transylvania."

Once an ocean tidal basin, the unique surface of the salt flats began to form at the end of the last ice age, when the waters of ancient Lake Bonneville began to recede. Covering nearly a third of Utah at one time, and roughly the size of Lake Michigan, the lake was nearly 1,000 feet deep in an area near the Great Salt Lake. Water slowly evaporated over time and minerals, including gypsum and halite (table salt), were left in the soil. Racing on the salt began in the early 1900s, with Ab Jenkins, the twenty-fourth mayor of Salt Lake City, setting speed records in the 1930s in the Mormon Meteor.

But in the 1960s, jet cars, simply put, were a totally different breed of animal. In fact, the decade opened with tragedy. In the summer of 1960, Utah garage owner Athol Graham tumbled and flipped across the salt at more than 300 mph while behind the wheel of his handmade City of Salt Lake jet car. Graham later died as a result of his injuries.

Paula Murphy's first record-setting experience at the Bonneville Salt Flats came behind the wheel of a Studebaker in October 1963, when she was part of a Studebaker group that included Andy Granatelli, his brothers Joe and Vince, and Barbara Nieland. The group set nearly 350 production car speed records on the salt. *LandSpeed Productions Research Library / Paula Murphy Collection*

"It looks easy because you are going down a straight line," said H. A. "Humpy" Wheeler, a Firestone rep at the time, best known as one of NASCAR's top promoters. "Those [jet] cars wanted to go all over the place. The horsepower in those engines was so tremendous and they have a torque that wants to throw the power in a certain direction.

"Now, in airplanes it was no problem because they compensated with a rudder and a stick and all the other things . . . with the car, well they never made a car to run a jet engine. So, this was all pioneering stuff at the time."

Graham's car, in fact, had been shaped from a B-29 belly tank and was powered by twelve-cylinder Allison aircraft engine capable of 3,000 horsepower.

"At Bonneville you don't steer," said George Calloway. He was on the salt that day in 1964 with Murphy and equipment pioneer Jim Deist, who was credited with designing and implementing the first "drag chute" for safely stopping cars at speed and for packing chutes for Arfons.

"If you try to steer that thing, you're going to loop it," Calloway added. "Whenever I worked the starting line, and I saw a rookie coming up, I would just say, 'Look pal, you're not going to steer this thing. You're just along for the ride.' They all move, and you just have to let them move and then they will come back. If you try to bring them back, you'll get yourself into trouble."

Record holder Danny Thompson, whose father, Mickey Thompson, stunned the speed world with a run of 406.06 mph behind the wheel of his hand-built, four-engine Challenger Streamliner in 1960 at Bonneville, couldn't agree more.

"You're definitely not supposed to try to oversteer it," said Danny Thompson, who set a wheel-driven piston-engine mark of his own at 448.757 mph in Challenger 2 at Bonneville in 2018, a car of his late father's design. "When things get sideways at Bonneville, you pull the parachute. What the parachute does is separate the center of pressure from the center of gravity, and it gives the car more stability and yaw. So, when it's sideways, [the parachute] will bring it back . . . hopefully, bring it back straight.

"The surface is always wet . . . always . . . and really slick," Thompson added. "I equate it to driving on snow."

And not unlike test pilots in experimental aircraft, it took a special kind of driver to take on the salt, especially when behind the wheel of these crudely built, fire-breathing jet cars. Not everyone was up to the task.

"There weren't many racers who would get in a jet dragster because they were so dangerous," Wheeler noted. "You didn't know where the hell they were going to go. She jumped in it like, 'OK, what's next?' It got a lot of people stirred up in her favor . . . she had no compunction about getting in one.

"I asked a number of Indy drivers in particular to go out and run cars at the Salt Flats and they just flat wouldn't do it," Wheeler added. "It was so dangerous. When you have a wreck there, you don't even find the body, you find pieces. That's how bad it is, and the people in racing know that. It didn't matter whether they were a sprint car driver or an IndyCar driver or a NASCAR driver, they knew to stay away from the Salt Flats."

And Murphy, who simply showed up and went fast, summed up the record-setting experience for the magazine: "I'll tell you how it felt . . . like I was hanging out over the edge of the whole wide world with everything rushing up at me. I could catch those yellow 'mile' signs as I went by, but I had no idea what they said."

Later for *USAC News*, Murphy added, "It felt like sitting on the edge of the world and flying through space."

"When I pulled the lever for the parachute on the first run, it dragged in the water, so a wet parachute isn't the greatest thing to pack and rely on, but it worked on the return," Murphy said. "Nobody showed much concern for me, so I didn't really realize that I could kill myself in this thing, but I thought, 'What's one more pass?'"

The feat, which lasted a grand total of twenty minutes, landed Murphy—who was quickly dubbed "The Fastest Woman on Wheels"—on magazine covers, with more driving opportunities, and eventually, after an extended milestone-filled drag racing career, into the Motorsports Hall of Fame of America.

"It certainly gave me a lot of notoriety and publicity," Murphy said. "It helped my career . . . people must have wondered who'd be crazy enough to do such a dumb thing, 'Ah, there she is in living color.'"

Granatelli certainly had found a bit of a sweet spot for publicity on the salt flats for both Studebaker and STP, hoping that in addition to elevating Murphy, the publicity would draw more

Scoring a "Speed Kings" trading card in 1966 helped launch Paula Murphy beyond the racing world and into pop culture.
Prescott Speed Kings Card No. 7 / Erik Arneson Collection

sponsors and support to his marketing efforts, but the money didn't follow.

"Andy was a piece of work," Wheeler said. "If anybody could get a sponsor for something, he could. He was a promoter and a genius at all that. He had a tremendous knack for getting publicity . . . a lot of what he did was about getting on the front page instead of the third page.

"The problem when you go to the jet cars is you couldn't get an auto manufacturer involved because they don't make jet cars," Wheeler said. "Even the tire companies were a little reluctant to get in it. Keeping tires on those things was unbelievably difficult."

However, not everyone was framing Murphy's record-setting performance in the most flattering ways. The sports world was still an all-boys club for the most part, especially among those covering events of the day. Sadly, writers for *Sports Illustrated*'s Scorecard put their 1960s chauvinism on full display, doing their best to trivialize Murphy's accomplishment:

> The first woman ever to drive a car at more than 200 miles an hour is a pretty brunette, 29, a divorcee and mother of an 11-year-old boy. She is also uncompromisingly feminine. Like most of her sex she changes her mind, drastically and often.

Of note, multiple media sources of the time, including the one above, cite Murphy's age as twenty-nine at the time of the Avenger run—most likely the result of a little Granatelli spin, but possibly a simple historically repeated mistake.

A Studebaker telegram located in the Granatelli Collection archives dated June 16, 1964, from Granatelli to Murphy offers a bit of a convincing hint:

> Congratulations on your 29th birthday. May you always be under 30 – Andy

So, at the actual age of thirty-six, Murphy had performed beyond anyone's expectations at Bonneville, but it certainly came as no surprise to her: "My competitive drive just comes naturally to me . . . either you have it or you don't."

"Altogether, it was a real hairy experience," Murphy said later in *Modern Rod* magazine. "I was plenty scared. But I did it and I did it all right. I guess I do these things because I can do them well— better than most women—maybe better than any other woman."

The truth of the matter was that Paula Murphy setting a land-speed record at the Bonneville Salt Flats was the result of a unique and perfect storm of patriotism, American ingenuity, timing, and corporate competition coming together in mid-1960s America. With the high-profile Space Race rapidly escalating because of the

At this celebration of one of the hundreds of records set by the Studebaker team in 1963, there was no hiding the fact that it was all about publicity for the car maker. *LandSpeed Productions Research Library / Paula Murphy Collection*

Cold War rivalry between the United States and the Soviet Union, cosmonaut Valentina Tereshkova became the first woman in space just a little over a year before Murphy's run in Avenger. And just a few years earlier, in 1961, President John F. Kennedy challenged the country with his, "Ask not what your country can do for you—ask what you can do for your country" speech, pushing Americans to contribute in some way to the public good.

"This was 'Gee Whiz' America," said racer, author, and land-speed historian "LandSpeed" Louise Noeth. "Gee Whiz, we could do that . . . Gee Whiz, I think I can do that . . . when you did it and a potential sponsor saw you, it was, Gee Whiz, how'd he do that."

"And I think that's where Paula was at the time," Noeth continued. "She didn't come to any of these cars with, 'Oh, I'm never going to be able to do this.' She always came to a car with 'Let's see what I can do with this one.' It was never an 'if,' it was always a 'what.' That was and is part of Paula's DNA."

Wheeler also acknowledged Murphy's unique blend of talent and guts.

"I recently asked a number of F1 drivers and IndyCar drivers from the sixties this question: 'What did it feel like at the start of the race during that time when there was so much death and dismemberment? How do you put that out of your mind?' And they all said the same thing—'We just did.'

"Some people can't do that; very few people can do it," Wheeler added. "She obviously was one of them. What she did that day on the salt was pretty darn incredible."

Murphy's "let's see what I can do" approach, a collectively competitive US attitude, poor conditions at Bonneville, and a highly energized corporate battle to sell tires and automotive products all came together at the right place at the right time.

"It had rained and snowed the night before [at Bonneville] and the place was in terrible shape," Murphy said in *Hot Rod* magazine. "The Arfons crew was there with their land speed record car, but because of the poor weather, they weren't able to run it then. So, they asked me to come up, as all the USAC people were already there, and rather than waste their money, they brought me up for a second run."

For Arfons and the team, the move was, at least in part, an effort to keep things actively rolling. You couldn't just "hold the salt."

"When racing began at Bonneville in earnest—with the British and everybody in the thirties and the forties—there were schedules for racing on the salt," Noeth said. "The Department of the Interior [before there was a Bureau of Land Management] ultimately didn't have the staff to regulate who was going to be on the Bonneville Salt Flats on what day and what time. The Salt Lake City Chamber of Commerce, which had a vested interest in the racing, put their hand up and said, 'We'll do it for you . . . we'll do that and we'll have the state road guys go and prepare the courses, so you don't have to worry about public land getting screwed up.' That's the way time on the salt was managed from the thirties to the mid-seventies.

"If you wanted to race at Bonneville, you called the Salt Lake City Chamber of Commerce," Noeth added. "But it came with the caveat, that all the days you scheduled, you'd better be actively racing. You couldn't just squat . . . all the competitors would be waiting."

Thus, the rush to get Murphy to the salt in time to keep the team in its scheduled slot. *Auto Topics* reported that she arrived in Salt Lake City around 8:00 p.m. local time on November 11. They took a rental car to Wendover and arrived at 11:00 p.m., met with Arfons at a Wendover café, and papers were signed close to 2:00 a.m. Paula and the team were up and ready to make their historic run at 8:00 a.m. on November 12.

While not directly part of the Bonneville tire wars, Murphy's historic run inspired additional opportunities for women to make record-chasing runs on the salt. In 1965, Craig Breedlove and his wife, Lee, were on the salt with their Spirit of America machine, backed by Goodyear, which also supported Walt Arfons. Firestone had teamed with Walt's brother, Art, who put Betty Skelton—the 1956 record holder in a Corvette—on the salt, behind the wheel of his Cyclops jet car. Both Breedloves set land-speed records (LSR); Lee's four-wheel mark of 308.56 mph in her husband's J79 jet-engine Spirit of America Sonic 1 is still recognized as the USAC speed record. Murphy, Breedlove, and Skelton's runs all were timed by FIA-sanctioned USAC personnel on a surveyed and certified course that included course stewards who monitored the entire process.

"That's why they put Lee Breedlove in the car," Noeth said. "That's why they had the AMX that Lee and Craig ran. That's why they brought the Shelby Daytona, because that was Goodyear using the time that had been blocked for publicity and for other types of motorsports, just to keep their name in the news cycle—

**Paula Murphy with STP boss Andy Granatelli (left) and
Studebaker president Byers A. Burlingame (right). The
relationship between Granatelli and the STP brand lasted
throughout Murphy's racing career and the time she set
automotive records.** *LandSpeed Productions Research Library /
Paula Murphy Collection*

newspapers, wire services, and a little bit of TV here and there. It
was all about selling rubber."

Skelton, who piloted Cyclops at the behest of Firestone, pushed
for more power behind her efforts on the Salt. From *Hemmings
Motor News*:

> In 1965, Skelton returned to Bonneville for the opportunity
> to drive Art Arfons' Cyclops jet car for Firestone tires. Her
> first pass on the salt was disappointing, and Skelton quickly
> complained that Arfons hadn't given her enough throttle to
> make a truly fast run. Modifications to the J-47 jet engine
> were made for the return trip, where Skelton clocked a speed

of 315.6 mph, good enough for a two-way average of 277.52 mph and a new woman's land speed record.

Ultimately, that's what landed the trio of Murphy, Breedlove, and Skelton opportunities to go fast and show their mettle—the possibility of drawing the attention of potential sponsors like STP and the ongoing need for Firestone and Goodyear to hold the salt. And all three delivered, despite being handicapped by their teams—Murphy being told not to use the afterburner, and Breedlove and Skelton both obviously tuned down as a safety measure, and most certainly to ensure their speeds came nowhere close to the men. In her 2021 book, *Images of Modern America: Bonneville's Women of Land Speed Racing,* Noeth noted, "Momentous will be the day when the world speed crown becomes a tiara."

The ongoing "jet car wars" continued to draw national and international attention. Highlighting the underlying "tire wars," Olsen's *Sports Illustrated* piece "Duel on the Salt" showcased the intensity of the salt-filled clash just one year after Murphy's run:

> All through last winter and spring, while Firestone's publicity campaign continued, there were rumors about the cars the two [Arfons] brothers were readying for the new year. Goodyear was said to be in a state of corporate apoplexy over the land-speed record and wanted it back whatever the cost. One could understand the annoyance. As a Goodyear spokesman reviewed the 1964 racing season at Bonneville: "Every time we scheduled a press conference to exploit a new land-speed record on Goodyears, Art Arfons'd go out and break our record for Firestone. Every time we'd run a big ad about a record, Art'd break our record while the ad was still on the streets. It made us look silly and it made us mad, especially when you consider that Art blew tires twice and we never had a trace of tire trouble on our own runs. They had the trouble

and as a reward they get one year of good publicity. We had no tire trouble at all, and we get one year of zip, nothing.

"It was a magnificent time back then on the salt," Wheeler said. "When *Reader's Digest* [did] their version of the centerfold on the Russian roulette at the salt flats with Arfons and Breedlove, that was big stuff. *Reader's Digest* at that time was a big deal."

In fact, it was the tire companies funding nearly all major LSR efforts of the day.

"Absolutely, one hundred percent of it," Wheeler confirmed. "For Art Arfons, it was one hundred percent of his money. For Breedlove, it was probably seventy-five percent of the money. So, the tire companies were like, 'Here's what we're going to do. Here's what we want you to do. Roll on.'"

The publicity battle over which tire was on the world's fastest car reached epic levels, much of which played out in the pages of *Life Magazine.*

Paula Murphy and fellow sports car racer Barbara Nieland at the Bonneville Salt Flats. Nieland set twenty-six marks of her own as part of the Studebaker assault on speed. *LandSpeed Productions Research Library / Paula Murphy Collection*

Tire Wars

- In 1963, a Goodyear two-page ad touted "407 MPH on Goodyear Tires," noting Craig Breedlove "brought the record back to America," and promising Goodyear engineers at Bonneville would shape the future of tires on "your car."

- In 1965, Firestone's two-page ad in *Life* celebrated Jim Clark's Indianapolis 500 win, with photos of other Firestone drivers, including Art Arfons.

- In the December 1965 issue of *Life*, Goodyear was back with Craig and Lee Breedlove—"Faster Car, Fastest Man (600.60), Fastest Woman (308.56)."

For Walt Arfons, however, it was Granatelli and Studebaker's STP money funding the lion's share of the Murphy effort, hoping to capitalize on the red-hot media spotlight on the salt. According to archived STP documents in the Granatelli Collection, Arfons was to receive a base payment of $2,500 for giving Murphy a spot behind the wheel—if she achieved an average speed above 200 mph. Arfons would receive an additional $50 for every mile per hour over 200 mph, up to a total of $5,000. The agreement included exclusive sponsor status for STP, as well as use of the car for promotional events.

Arfons received a total of $3,850, along with a few gifts with a familiar logo. An accompanying handwritten note from the archives directed a few STP promotional items to be sent along to Arfons, including five hundred Novi STP decals, a size 38 STP jacket, six cases of gasoline treatment, six cases of STP oil treatment, six cases of Diesel Blitz, one hundred pocket protectors with STP pens, and twelve STP T-shirts of various sizes.

Paula Murphy's driveway stood out in the neighborhood with her new title, record speed, and, of course, an STP sticker on full display. *LandSpeed Productions Research Library / Paula Murphy Collection*

Amid the Bonneville tire wars, Granatelli seized an amazing promotional opportunity and the right person to pull it off. Paula Murphy showed up at the salt on November 12, 1964, jumped in a car she had never laid eyes on—a volatile jet-powered car created by an industrious Ohio feed mill operator—and made two passes in less-than-ideal racing conditions. The result: "The Fastest Woman on Wheels."

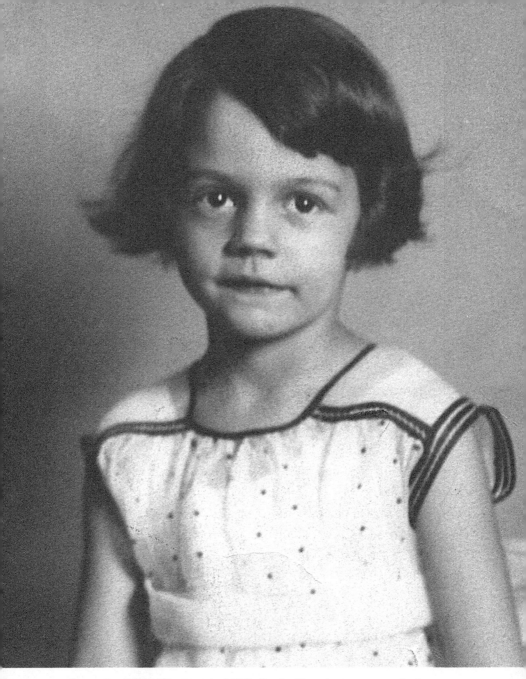

Born Paula Muhlhauser in 1928, Paula Murphy grew up during the Great Depression, but found no shortage of adventure on and around Lake Erie, winning sailboat races and becoming an accomplished equestrian as a teen. *LandSpeed Productions Research Library / Paula Murphy Collection*

Chapter 2

Origins of Speed

"Road racing is largely overlooked today in the annals of California's motorsports history. . . . But from the early 1950s to the mid–1960s, the sport flared brightly, attracting tens of thousands of people to race events. Road racing had everything: action, danger, exotic cars, star drivers, all taking place within the beautiful scenery of Southern California."
—MotorTrend *magazine*

Preparing for her first race, twelve-year-old Paula Murphy knew she was relying on older, more well-worn equipment than some of her competition, but she made no excuses and fearlessly took her place on the starting line.

Minutes later, the Ohio youngster was celebrating her first racing victory. She had taken first place in a 1940 Silver Skates Ice Carnival speed skating event in downtown Cleveland.

"I borrowed my mother's old skates . . . she had speed skates, the ones with the long blades," Murphy said. "I won the first race I ever competed in—ice skating."

A near-perfect case study in nature versus nurture, Murphy's early life experiences most certainly altered her trajectory toward a life defined by speed, competition, and more than a little risk. Then again, maybe she was simply born to go fast, shattering stereotypical boundaries along the way.

Born June 16, 1928, to tool designer Paul Muhlhauser and his wife Libbie Augusta Kuchenbecker (Muhlhauser) a full fourteen years after the couple was married, Murphy was raised during the Great Depression in a three-room apartment on a main street in Cleveland, one of the country's fastest growing and most vibrant cities during the Roaring Twenties. The modest apartment had a small utilitarian kitchen, one bedroom, and a living room that sported, of all things, a pull-down Murphy Bed where Paula would often sleep.

Libbie, who was working as an X-ray technician just a few years after the technology was in general hospital use, became a stay-at-home mother, but it was Murphy's father, Paul, who took on more of the nurturing role, reading to his daughter and spending time with her nearly every evening.

"I don't know what I would have done without my Dad," Murphy said. "My parents bought me the *My Book House* series—really nice big books for kids with all sorts of different stories. I always used to say 'Read to me, Daddy! Read to me!' And, even after a long day at work, he would read and read and read to me. I loved my Mom, but Dad was perfect."

Although money in the Muhlhauser household was tight, as it was for most Americans of the era, there was no lack of speed and adventure in Murphy's early life, with much of her youth spent on the expansive waters of Lake Erie.

"I was practically raised on a sailboat," Murphy said. "My Dad,

Much of Paula Murphy's youth was spent on a sailboat, as her father, Paul, built boats and competed as part of the Cleveland Yachting Club. *LandSpeed Productions Research Library / Paula Murphy Collection*

who built several of our boats by hand, and Mom took me along nearly every time they went out, except when he was racing."

Members of the Cleveland Yachting Club, the Muhlhausers competed annually in the Inter-Lake Yachting Association Regatta at Put-in-Bay, Ohio, on the northwest corner of Lake Erie. Murphy's participation began as a crew member on two-person Star Class boats.

"Getting into racing was more about being around the guys I knew at the yacht club who had boats but often didn't have anyone to crew for them," Murphy explained. "So, I raised my hand, and I eventually got to be quite the crewperson. Occasionally, guys would let me sail the boat during a race, and that's what got me started.

"As a crewperson, when the boat was changing direction, I'd move the jib, the little sail in front to pick up wind," Murphy said. "Oftentimes, if the breeze was stout, I hung my rear over the side to level the boat to help balance the boat. I also made sure all the lines were secure. It kept me busy . . . and usually wet."

By her late teens and into her early twenties, Murphy was racing, and winning, on her own. "At Put-in-Bay, there was a ladies K Class catboat race," Murphy said. "A catboat is a sailboat with a single mast carrying only one sail. It was an old boat even back then, but I won almost every year I competed."

In addition to sailing, Murphy was an active equestrian during her years at Lakewood High School, attending summer day camp

Never far from Lake Erie throughout her childhood, Paula Murphy (left) crewed and raced sailboats at Put-in-Bay, winning in a K Class catboat. *LandSpeed Productions Research Library / Paula Murphy Collection*

at a Cleveland landmark, Parker's Ranch, owned and operated by famous trick rider Adele von Ohl Parker in North Olmstead. Parker, a protégé of Buffalo Bill Cody and a rider in his famed Buffalo Bill's Wild West Show, also traveled the vaudeville circuit, starring in several shows, including Cheyenne Frontier Days. She also made multiple appearances with Ringling Bros. and Barnum & Bailey Circus.

According to Case Western Reserve University's *Encyclopedia of Cleveland History*:

> Parker's first public appearance as a daredevil rider was in 1905 at the Hippodrome Theater in New York City. There, riding astride her horse Delmar, she performed an act in which she plunged from a high platform into a tank of water below. Her act captured the attention of the local media, which noted that she was one of the first women on the East Coast to ride astride her horse rather than side saddle. From 1907 to 1909, Parker appeared with Buffalo Bill's Wild West show, performing acts like picking up a gold coin from the ground while on a horse at full gallop and commanding her horse to rear up and march on its two hind legs.

"I used to go to day camp to ride during summer vacation," Murphy said. "This old, rattly Ford station wagon with the wooden sides would pull up every day and take me to Parker's Ranch . . . I'd spend the whole day riding at Cleveland Metroparks; it was huge, with riding trails all over the place."

"She was a real character," Murphy said of Parker, who set a strong example of a woman competing and succeeding in a traditionally male pursuit. "She always wore a cowboy hat and was very strict as an instructor, but absolutely everyone loved her."

Murphy, again, was fearless in her approach. "I used to do 'fender drags' and 'flying dismounts' . . . I participated in horse shows. . . . We did a lot with horses, and I even had a horse of my own for a while."

Staying close to home, Murphy started college at Bowling Green State University south of Toledo. Following her freshman year, the family moved to Cincinnati when her father transferred within the Cleveland Automatic Machine Company. He had started at six-and-a-half cents an hour and would go on to spend the remainder of his career there.

Murphy transferred to the University of Cincinnati and graduated in 1949 with a degree in health and physical education. With hopes of becoming a teacher, the only offers that came her way were from out of state and Paula was more comfortable staying closer to home.

"I was also offered a commission—we were still in World War II at the time—in the new Special Women's Medical Service Corps," Murphy said. "I would have been trained as a physical therapist at Johns Hopkins, but there again, I was concerned about moving away from Mom and Dad, and I didn't go."

Murphy eventually went to work for the Community Chest as a social worker. The first Community Chest, later the United Way, was formed in 1913 in Cleveland. Just two years later, she accepted a job in the General Electric Relocation Office, where she helped new employees find places to live in the Cincinnati area.

Marrying GE colleague Dan Murphy, she gave birth to their son, Danny, in 1953, and the young family moved to California to advance her husband's career in aerospace sales when Danny was just three months old. Paula took a position with Marquardt, an aerospace engineering firm in North Hollywood, where she spent several years working on the Saturn S-IVB missile project as an engineering aide, creating visual representations from rocket test data.

Murphy also purchased a new car—a 1954 MG TF—as her daily driver. After all, it was Southern California, an area of the

Paula Murphy, shown here in front of the Kappa Alpha Theta house (back row, second from left), attended Lakewood High School in the suburbs of Cleveland before moving on to Bowling Green State University and the University of Cincinnati, where she earned a degree in Health and Physical Education.
LandSpeed Productions Research Library / Paula Murphy Collection

country known for hot rods and auto racing. What color? "Red, of course," Murphy said with a chuckle.

The purchase wound up adding strain on a marriage that already wasn't working out. Dan Murphy wanted more control. Paula wasn't the type of person to allow it, saying, "I just couldn't stand him any longer."

Divorced in 1956, Danny remembers his father being in the picture off and on until he was about ten. "And then he moved away, and we had no idea where he was after that—no child support, no contact, no nothing."

A year earlier, In January 1955, tragedy had hit the Muhlhauser family when Paula's parents were involved in a serious automobile accident back in Cincinnati. Paula's father, Paul, was born in 1882 and despite Paula's increased interest and participation in racing, he never learned to drive, and instead took a streetcar to work every day. Libbie was at the wheel of the family's brand-new Ford station wagon (seatbelts were not yet included in cars) when she was run off the road and into a retaining wall, suffering severe injuries upon impact with the steering wheel. Paul, on the passenger side, broke through the windshield with his head. Paul survived. Libbie did not. A year or so after the accident that killed her mother, Murphy, now a single mother, brought her father out to California to live with her and help with raising Danny.

How It All Began

Coworker and former professional figure skater Jean Calvin was an automotive writer for *Sportscar Graphic* and an SCCA driver. Calvin invited Murphy to attend the 1956 Santa Barbara Memorial Day Race.

"Through my job, I met several people who were big into road racing—sports car racing," Murphy added. "And they said, 'You've got to go to the races with us.' Finally, I went with them, and I was like, uh, this is like watching the grass grow."

Murphy joined the Women's Sports Car Club, a service organization that worked at SCCA races, doing everything from timing slips to ticket sales, and continued to attend local races. Things got a little more interesting, however, when Murphy got behind the wheel for the first time.

"I met a guy who had an Alfa, and he said, 'Why don't you drive my car in the ladies' races?' and I said I'd give it a try."

In 1961, she shared the Adam-Mitchell Special 1600 with driver Scooter Patrick five times, winning twice and finishing second three times in the ride built from remnants of a Porsche 550.

For a story for The American Hot Rod Foundation, writer Tony Thacker tracked Murphy's sports car efforts: "The first entry I

Murphy, clowning around with racing pal Jean Calvin.

*LandSpeed Productions Research Library / Paula Murphy
Collection*

could find was January 31, 1959, when she raced an Alfa Romeo
Giulietta Spider for John E. English. She did okay, but by 1961–62
she was in her stride and recorded several first and many second
places. Mostly she was driving the Adam-Mitchell Special but her
list of rides included Porsche 550, 356 and a 718 RSK entered by
Vasek Polak."

Polak, a prominent Manhattan Beach car dealer and racer, was
considered the local Porsche authority and regularly fielded and
tuned teams with multiple drivers, including Murphy.

He went on to prepare entries for Jack MacAfee, Ken Miles,
Jerry Titus, Roger Penske, and others. After winning the Ladies
division of the seventeenth Annual Santa Barbara Road Races in
May 1962, Murphy was one of three Polak-tuned entries to win

in the Pomona Road Race at the Los Angeles Fairgrounds in July. Murphy piloted the Porsche RSK in the ten-lap Ladies category.

Not bad, considering a headline in the *Van Nuys News and Valley Green Sheet* screamed in all caps:

WOMAN DRIVER – EGAD! – TO ENTER SPORTS CAR MEET

While almost exclusively racing sports cars during this time, Murphy did get behind the wheel of other cars when opportunities arose. In August 1962, she won an eight-lap Pacific Raceway Association (PRA) women's stock car race at Saugus Stadium, a ⅓-mile racetrack in Saugus, Santa Clarita, driving an Oldsmobile owned by Rob Parker.

"My first race in the Alfa was at the Pomona Fairgrounds," Murphy recalled. "We'd take off down the drag strip, go left under the bridge, and they had a course laid out in the parking lot. It was a fun course. They lumped over- and under-1500cc, production, and modified together into one race," Murphy continued. "My first race, I won first in production under 1500 and I thought to myself, 'Wow, I can do this.'"

Racing at familiar California tracks like Santa Barbara, Torrey Pines, Palm Springs, and Riverside, the highlight of her sports car career came behind the wheel of a 3-liter Ferrari Testa Rossa, a car she shared with driver Chuck Towers at the Riverside Grand Prix in October 1960.

According to an article in the *Los Angeles Times*, Murphy beat out Hollywood's Betty Shutes "when the latter's Porsche came up with no second gear."

"I won my first overall in the Ferrari, a thrill to drive even though it was right-side steer and you had to shift with your left hand, which was something I had never done before," Murphy said. "I had no practice in the thing—nothing. With the power I had, however, I walked away from everybody. It was a piece of cake."

The rivalry with Shutes continued around the circuit, coming to a head at the Time-Mirror Grand Prix in January 1961.

According to the *Los Angeles Times*, "Betty and Paula, in a wild duel of Porsches, swapped the lead four times in a tight race before they collided on turn three when both girls tried to squeeze through the tricky turn at the same time."

The incident happened with Murphy leading, but despite both cars remaining in the race with minor damage following the contact, Murphy lost quite a bit of track position and Shutes went on to an apparent victory.

A true competitor since her early days on Lake Erie, Murphy launched an official protest, which was upheld, scoring driver Barbara Windhorst at the winner and Murphy in second.

In 1961, driving the Porsche Special, she scored a class win in January in Palm Springs and later took an overall class win at Stockton Field in an event sponsored by the Lions Club.

"I was starting to get the feeling I could do things that I could not have done ten years prior to that," Murphy continued. "I even raced a couple of races with the men and did pretty well." According to the Racing Sports Cars (RSC) archive, Murphy competed in twenty-five events between 1959 and 1962, finishing all but one and collecting five wins (eight additional class wins), five poles, and seven top-three finishes.

At the urging of Calvin, Murphy, who had run a divisional mileage rally in California, took on her first Mobilgas Economy Run in 1961, ultimately completing eight—running twice for Chevy, once with Ford, and five times with Buick. The economy runs, sanctioned by the SCCA, were designed to determine fuel efficiency numbers on public roads under normal driving conditions.

In a Marquardt company newsletter, they celebrated Murphy's success in the 1961 Mobil Mileage Rally, where she won divisional honors in the "four-passenger, over 1,600cc" class behind the wheel of a Citroën ID19. Murphy averaged 35.69 miles per gallon over the 300-mile course. The course covered a route from downtown Los Angeles into five counties and through forty-four cities and proved to be a good warmup for the longer run.

In 1961, the 2,560.7-mile course ran from Los Angeles to Tucson to Roswell, New Mexico, to Dallas to Little Rock, Arkansas, to

Paula Murphy's introduction to motorsports came when a coworker took her to see local SCCA races in Southern California. Beginning in 1959, she started showing her mettle behind the wheel and was competing in a wide variety of rides, including this Porsche Spyder (pictured at right). *LandSpeed Productions Research Library / Paula Murphy Collection*

St. Louis, Missouri, to Chicago. With a record-setting entry list of sixty-seven cars, nearly every American make joined the action.

"It was a really fun event," Murphy recalled. "I was working at the time, but they'd let me off or else I'd take two weeks' vacation. First, we'd do a little practice run. We'd use the log from the previous year's run, and we'd redo that run; maybe the whole way, maybe only halfway."

With Calvin as her navigator, the effort had very little to do with going fast, and in fact they worked extra hard not to go too fast.

"Everything was timed to the minute, so you've got to be right on the dot," Murphy said. "We had a little handheld calculator, and I drew charts as to how fast we should be going at certain points, and we could never exceed the speed limit. We had an observer riding with us to make sure we didn't do anything like tuck up

Paula Murphy hit her sports car stride in 1961–62, recording
several first-place and many second-place finishes. Often driving
the Adam-Mitchell Special, her list of rides included a Porsche
550, 356, and a 718 RSK. *LandSpeed Productions Research
Library / Paula Murphy Collection*

behind a truck, because a truck can pull you along pretty good,"
Murphy continued. "That was a no-no. It was a new event for me,
and it cleared the dust so to speak."

A 1967 issue of *Drag Racing* magazine chronicled some of Murphy's
economy run exploits:

> In 1961, she navigated her first run for Sunnie Baker in a
> Chevrolet on a trip that terminated in Chicago. In 1962,
> Paula drove herself, and had a Chevrolet again, this time
> winding up third in her class on a trip that ended at Detroit.
> In 1963, she switched to Ford and wound up second to last,
> also ending at Detroit . . . In 1964, the first year that she
> drove a Buick, the trip went to New York and Buick won
> three of the four classes they were entered in. Paula was in
> the fourth class.

In 1965, she drove a V-6 Special on a trip to New York that ended for Paula in a hospital in St. Louis when her back gave her trouble. She spent six days there while her navigator finished the race. In 1966, the Mobil Run went to Boston and Paula again drove a Buick V-6 Special to a second-place finish. In 1967, the Mobil Run went to Detroit and again at the wheel of a V-6 Special for Buick. She wound up No. 3 in Class C with an average of 21.92 mpg.

After having forged important relationships across the industry with the economy runs and having enjoyed some success on the Southern California tracks, including Pomona and Riverside, the phone rang for Murphy in 1963. Bill Dredge, the *Los Angeles Times* auto editor from 1959 to 1962, was on the other end of the line.

"He said, 'How would you like to drive a car coast to coast, border to border, and set some speed records along the way?'" recalled Murphy, then an engineering aid working on the Saturn missile project. "He also asked me if I could recommend another woman racer to drive with me, and I suggested Barbara Nieland."

Since leaving the *Times*, Dredge had moved on to a public relations role, and some credit him with bringing together Andy Granatelli and Studebaker/STP. A short time later, Granatelli called Murphy and Nieland, later referring to the pair as the "Flying Housewives." With North Hollywood automotive engineer, technical writer, and cross-country driving expert Bill Carroll added to the group, the team piloted a Studebaker Avanti coast to coast for a series of records, including a transcontinental mark from Los Angeles to New York in forty-nine hours, thirty-seven minutes.

After the LA to New York run, the group rested for a couple of days before driving from New York to Tijuana, Mexico, via Dallas; then to Vancouver, Canada, and back to Tijuana, setting multiple records by journey's end. Billed as an automotive performance and Sears tire test, the car, the Studebaker Avanti Sports Coupe, was selected from the production line by USAC chief steward Joe Petrali and Sears All-State Guardsmen nylon tires were selected from Sears stocks.

According to a *Long Beach Press-Telegram* article by automotive editor Art Stephan, the nearly 9,000-mile cross-country odyssey, which began on August 23, 1963, took a total of 150 hours, 55 minutes of road time, including stops for fuel that averaged just under three minutes each. These were the only stops made, for the drivers did their eating on the run, and the crew suspended operations at each terminal point for twenty-four hours of rest before proceeding on the next leg of the run.

At the urging of friend and fellow racer Jean Calvin, Paula Murphy took on the first of her eight Mobilgas Economy Runs in 1961, running twice for Chevy, once with Ford, and five times with Buick. The economy runs, sanctioned by the SCCA, were designed to determine fuel efficiency numbers on public roads under normal driving conditions. *LandSpeed Productions Research Library / Paula Murphy Collection*

RESULTS 1968 MOBIL ECONOMY RUN

4TH DAY   INDIANAPOLIS   TOP-OFF ST. CHARLES, MO. MILES TO DATE 2013.9

DAILY RESULTS ARE
FROM WAKEENEY, KAN.   TO   ST. CHARLES   MILES   529.4

AVG MPG ALL CARS		AVG MPG MEN		AVG MPG WOMEN	
Cumulative	Daily	Cumulative	Daily	Cumulative	Daily
19.2061	18.9677	19.0431	18.7971	19.9747	19.7834

NO	PL	MPG CUMULATIVE	TODAY'S MPG	MODEL	DRIVER
CLASS A		**COMPACT SIX CYLINDER CARS**			
4	3	22.8586	22.8963	Corvair 500	Gordon Madison
6	6	22.0401	22.2375	Dodge Dart 170	Mary Ann Foss
19	7	21.1458	20.9287	Falcon 170	Bill Levy
33	5	22.7199	22.4286	Mustang 2 + 2	Kay Kimes
18	4	22.7538	22.4266	Valiant	Bob Cahill
31	2	23.3732	22.7283	Barracuda	Jerry Gross
9	1	24.1912	23.4849	Rambler Rogue	Les Viland
CLASS B		**COMPACT EIGHT CYLINDER CARS**			
1	3	19.6514	19.5030	Chevy II Nova	Mary Hauser
41	2	19.6587	19.0352	Mustang 2 + 2	Fran Foster
21	4	19.6314	18.7455	Valiant	Bob Checkley
40	1	20.0902	19.5566	Barracuda 318	Jack Kirkpatrick
2	5	16.3758	16.2374	Javelin	Tommy Thomas
CLASS C		**INTERMEDIATE SIZE SIX CYLINDER CARS**			
12	4	19.3079	19.0648	Chevelle 300	Ed Miller
29	1	22.8397	22.0615	Fairlane	Ginny Sims
36	2	22.6553	22.5504	Mercury Montego	Al Johnson
14	3	22.1210	21.2819	Plymouth Belvedere	Carl Diehl
CLASS D		**INTERMEDIATE SIZE EIGHT CYLINDER CARS**			
25	5	18.5469	18.6353	Buick Special	John Rich
23	6	17.9706	17.7630	Chevelle Malibu	Dr. Tom Evans
16	1	20.6758	20.1587	Dodge Coronet	Shirley Shahan
37	4	19.1651	18.4805	Ford Torino GT	Darrell Droke
32	3	19.4990	19.0208	Mercury Montego	Ronnie Duman
8	7	17.0600	16.9988	Olds F-85	Mel Alsbury, Jr.
39	2	20.5116	19.7455	Plymouth Belvedere	Scott Harvey
28	8	16.9051	16.9943	Pontiac Tempest	Don Francisco
CLASS E		**LOW PRICE EIGHT CYLINDER CARS—STANDARD SIZE**			
10	1	18.8655	18.7048	Chevy Impala SS	Don Royer
20	4	17.4066	16.7993	Chevy Caprice	C. K. Enoch
11	3	17.9780	17.7875	Ford Custom	John Allen
7	2	18.4095	18.0315	Plymouth Fury III	Bill Keller
CLASS F		**MEDIUM PRICE EIGHT CYLINDER CARS STANDARD SIZE**			
22	1	18.4679	18.7061	Buick LeSabre 400	Marta Retzlaff
15	4	17.3441	17.1558	Chrysler Newport	Jim Latham
17	2	18.4497	18.5801	Dodge Polara 318	Jim Wright
3	5	16.9192	16.9790	Mercury Monterey	Byron Froelich
~~26~~		~~WITHDRAWN~~		~~Olds Delmont 88~~	~~Diane Lowe~~
13	6	16.2945	16.5108	Olds Delta 88	Stan Raymond
35	3	17.9691	18.0687	Pontiac Catalina	Ted Block
CLASS G		**LUXURY CARS**			
5	3	16.4894	16.7817	Buick Electra 225	Paula Murphy
24	6	15.4778	15.3067	Cadillac	Pete Novotny
38	1	17.1474	17.0146	Chrysler New Yorker	Hart Fullerton
30	2	16.6990	16.8202	Olds 98	Mandy Williams
34	5	15.5696	16.6992	Thunderbird	Nelson Stacy
27	4	16.0094	15.8786	Olds Toronado	Tom Gillum, Jr.

68263

Murphy participated in multiple Mobil Economy Runs. This 1968
time sheet shows her leading the way in a Buick Electra 225
after a leg from Indianapolis to St. Charles, Missouri. *LandSpeed
Productions Research Library / Paula Murphy Collection*

According to an article in the *Los Angeles Times*, sleeping and eating presented challenges, as drivers took four-hour shifts.

"Metrecal [low-calorie powdered food] and baby food kept us going," Murphy said in the *Times*. "Sleep was catch-as-catch-can. We could sleep eight of every twenty-four hours in the back of the wagon . . . if you could sleep. I got about two hours at that time."

The average speed for the entire trip was 58.73 mph, with the best (average) speed of 60.31 mph obtained on the New York to San Diego leg.

Tires were carefully measured for tread wear along the way. The Avanti was lubricated and had its oil changed at each stop, but no additional service was permitted. The threesome followed a Studebaker Wagonaire that carried two servicemen, an alternate driver, and an alternate USAC official.

The wagon also carried a phone, and according to Carroll, the publicity opportunities were as important as the driving. "In one town, we asked the operator to connect us to the biggest radio station in town," Carroll said in a *Los Angeles Times* article. "She answered crisply, 'Sir, there's only ONE radio station in town.'"

"It was the most thrilling thing I've done in my life," Murphy said in the *Times* article. "I would never had considered quitting."

At the conclusion of the event, Granatelli and Sears tire representative Tom Filline teased a continuation of the testing at the famed Bonneville Salt Flats, with an eye toward speed and racing performance. Murphy was all in. And records would fall.

"We've been nursing that throttle for economy so long that we're itching for a chance to push it right through the floorboards," she said in the *Press-Telegram* article.

Later in that same year, with Granatelli flexing his Indianapolis Motor Speedway muscle and driver Eddie Sachs offering guidance and instruction, Paula Murphy scored another first on November 11, 1963.

Positioned as a tire test season for Granatelli's new dual-overhead cam supercharged V8-powered, STP-badged Studebaker Novi, Murphy was cleared to make three medium-paced laps around the iconic speedway, becoming the first woman to ever pilot a race car around the facility at speed.

"Andy showed a lot of faith in my abilities," Murphy said. "And I had all the trust in the world in him. He told me where to show up and what time to be there, and I went to work."

Granatelli had many nicknames throughout his storied career including "Mr. 500" and *Sports Illustrated* writer Bob Ottum's moniker, "the roundest known automotive pixie." Donald Davidson said Granatelli was "without a doubt, one of the most dominant and iconic personalities in the history of Indianapolis Motor Speedway." Granatelli and the STP brand were known for having the juice to get things done. And get it done they did.

Aware of what Paula Murphy was doing on the California sports car circuit, it was former *Los Angeles Times* auto editor Bill Dredge who connected her to Andy Granatelli. Dredge went on to handle public relations for STP, helping to shape and promote Murphy's career. *LandSpeed Productions Research Library / Paula Murphy Collection*

In an article for STP-sponsored *Auto Racing Magazine* titled, "Paula Murphy—As I See Her," Granatelli wrote:

> [In] less than an hour, I had persuaded the tire test crew, who had the privilege of the track, and Al Bloemker and Tony Hulman and Clarence Cagle, who really run the place, plus about a half dozen other people, that Paula should get a shot at immortality by driving an STP Novi, of all the impossible things, around the Indianapolis brickyard.
>
> It wasn't easy. The only other gal, within memory of man, to even tour the track at the wheel of a car was the late, great Amelia Earhart. Women, you know, aren't allowed in the pits, in Gasoline Alley or within a country mile of running a race car—let alone in the cockpit, out there hot lapping.

"They knew I would be the first . . . it almost took special dispensation from the Pope to allow me to do that," Murphy recalled. "What, a woman drive at Indy?"

The experience did not come without the prerequisite public relations preening and some performance restrictions on Granatelli's Novi-powered Studebaker, a car described by writer Deke Houlgate as, "that terrible, snarly, wall-banging Novi, the car that made the STP logo something special."

"They had me putting on lipstick and patting my hair and giving everyone goo-goo eyes for all the cameras," Murphy recalled. "[STP] told me to do it because they thought it would be cute, and I was like 'Oh, boy.' But I did what I was asked to do."

In a 1970 article for *Hot Rod Magazine*, Murphy noted: "The throttle was locked, and I was restricted to 100 mph and only three laps."

"One of [Granatelli's] brothers said, 'Oh, she'll never be able to shift that car,'" Murphy recalled.

Murphy took it as a challenge.

Paula Murphy drove quite a few Porsche entries, including this
RS-61, but her first overall win came in a 3-liter Ferrari Testa
Rossa. *LandSpeed Productions Research Library / Paula Murphy
Collection*

"The shifter was between my legs, and I thought, 'I can do that,'"
Murphy said. "They pushed me out and off I went. I got around
Turns One and Two, and I was heading down the back straight
and thought, 'Now, it's time to shift,' so I took both hands off the
steering wheel and took both hands and pulled the shifter down
and off I went . . . it was simple and I could have gone around that
track a few more times than they allowed me because it was so fun."

Despite the thrill of making a few laps, Murphy was defini-
tive in her responses to media questions about eventually racing in
the Indianapolis 500: a resounding no. And she remained resolute
in her decision years later when she returned to the speedway to

drive the pace car. When *New York Times* reporter Phil Pash asked her about possibly being the first woman to race in the 500, Paula confessed, "It won't be me. Because I'm not that crazy about driving open wheel cars. I don't mind if I am the only one on the track, but if there are going to be other cars out there with me, I want fenders and roofs and things like that. Maybe that's the stock car racer in me talking."

In a run that was billed as a "tire test," Paula Murphy was the first woman to turn laps at Indianapolis Motor Speedway, noting, "It almost took special dispensation from the Pope to allow me to do that." *LandSpeed Productions Research Library / Paula Murphy Collection*

Following the motorsports axiom of "race on Sunday, sell on Monday," STP got its money's worth out of Paula Murphy's Indianapolis laps. *LandSpeed Productions Research Library / Paula Murphy Collection*

The hesitancy was reinforced in the years following her solo runs around the famed track.

"I did do the laps at Indy, but there is no way you could have gotten me in one to race," Murphy said. "I didn't want anything to do with open wheel cars. The first year I went to Indy was in 1955 when [Bill] Vukovich was killed. I went back in 1964, and that's when [Eddie] Sachs and Dave McDonald were killed."

Part of the equation that wasn't talked about much was where she felt more welcome. Murphy noted in *Speed and Supercar* magazine that, "there's a little more resentment against a girl driving open cockpit cars around the ovals than there is in drag racing." For Murphy, it would be a future of reaction times and straight-line speed.

Life on the road often meant traveling to multiple tracks in a single week. Commanding as much as $1,000 an appearance, the Murphys and mechanic "Fat Jack" Bynum checked off tracks from California strips like Lions Drag Strip; to Midwest tracks like Great Lakes Dragaway, US 30 Drag Strip, and Dragway 42 in West Salem, Ohio; to East Coast hot spots like New Jersey's Atco Dragway. *Murphy Family Collection*

Chapter 3

Life's a Drag (1965–1970)

"'The Fastest Women on Wheels' is a title that long belonged to a pert brunette who is today one of the two best-known women in the field of drag racing. Paula Murphy has the most experience in sports car racing and has the best publicity because of her feats at the Bonneville Salt Flats but has made some serious inroads into the sport of brutal truths, drag racing."
—*Karen Nelson, 1967,* Drag Racing *magazine*

Murphy's record-setting time on the salt in Walt Arfons's jet car in 1964—under the brief jet-car tutelage of Akron, Ohio, drag racer Bob Tatroe—bore fruit just a few years later, as the newly crowned "Fastest Woman on Wheels" explored opportunities on California's quarter-mile drag strips.

Giving up the pure joy of driving exotics around tricky tracks throughout the Golden State was a tough sell, but there was money to be made on the hundreds of straight-line tracks around the country. With her headline-grabbing credentials and a tongue-in-cheek willingness to do a little gender flexing, Murphy scored an opportunity to tap into the lucrative career through a boyfriend who happened to work at a local Oldsmobile dealership.

In 1965, the Los Angeles and Orange County Oldsmobile Dealers Association planned to campaign a pair of Oldsmobile 442 muscle cars in the National Hot Rod Association (NHRA) Stock Eliminator category. Prepared by Mopar legend Dick Landy, the standard transmission version would be run by Ron Root with Murphy taking on the automatic sponsored by Guy Martin Oldsmobile.

Staying close to home in Southern California, Murphy ran in NHRA Division 7, the Pacific Division. The following year, she ran only half of the season, with the car often facing protests from competitors. Years later, she explained why:

"I had a sixty-six that [Landy] prepared and we ran C/Stock Automatic. We kept getting protested because he put in a four-speed station wagon transmission in the thing and it was really supposed to be just a three-speed. The Buicks had the four-speed, and they just killed us all the time. Then Landy put the four-speed in. They would say, 'I can hear another shift . . . We can hear another shift.' But the tech people never tore the transmission out of the thing, because it looked just like a regular three speed."

During the '66 season, Murphy crossed paths with the man known in drag racing circles as "Fat Jack." Jack Bynum, the rough-around-the-edges, supersized-personality mechanic was leaving the grounds at Irwindale Speedway with a couple of buddies when they noticed Murphy and one of her helpers from Landy's camp struggling to get the Olds back on its trailer.

Bynum and the others were quick to assist, and later that evening, Murphy and Bynum got to talking at the local racers' watering hole, the

Irwindale Inn, just south of the dragstrip. Bynum suggested the pair move to the fledgling Funny Car class, and the pitch worked. Murphy left her job as an engineering aid at Whitaker Controls and the pair became a fixture at tracks around the country for years to come.

Bynum, the Southern California wrench, instantly became a mentor and mechanic for Murphy. Fellow racer, Pat Foster, offered a description of Bynum for Draglist.com: "To say Jack was a genuine one-off man would be an understatement. He was the roughest talking SOB you'd ever want to meet and if you messed with him (or Miss Paula) you better 'Sit Low' for a few rounds. The exterior gave you no hint of the gentle giant inside his 250-pound frame. Jack was thought by many to not be the sharpest tool in the shed, but they were wrong."

Drag racing icon Don "The Snake" Prudhomme recalled crossing paths in his youth with the man they referred to as the "bully of Bob's" during the growing California car club cruising scene.

One of the early versions of Murphy's inaugural Funny Car effort, the Mustang takes to the track at famed Lions Drag Strip in Wilmington, California. *Erik Arneson Collection*

"I go way back with 'Fat Jack,'" said Prudhomme, who was ranked number three on the NHRA's Top 50 Drivers list. "We all used to hang out at Bob's Big Boy in Van Nuys, but I didn't really hang out with Jack because he was older than me and my buddies. We'd cruise through Bob's and he and a couple of his friends would be standing on the corner hurling nasty comments at us [and others] as we drove by.

"He thought we were from the San Fernando Bob's—a lot of those guys would cruise back and forth from San Fernando and Van Nuys. 'Fat Jack' would call us 'tamale gobblers,' and he was fucking bigger than me, so we all tried to avoid even looking at him—the bully of Bob's."

The pairing of the college-educated and stylish Murphy with the foulmouthed, brutish Bynum seemed unlikely, but the pair appeared to make it work.

"Here she is this nice, gentle gal and you've got this 'Fat Jack,'" Prudhomme said. "It always amazed me wondering how the hell he got to that point of tuning her car and running her car, but he did a pretty decent job apparently."

"Would Mom have been better off teamed with someone else?" Murphy's son, Danny, said. "Good chance that's a yes, but no one else was offering and she wanted to go racing and make a living."

A far cry from the smooth-handling sports cars she began racing with, Murphy's attraction to drag racing was not immediate.

"In the beginning, I didn't think drag racing looked like a lot of fun," Murphy said. "I mean, zip and it's over with. It's not like other forms of racing where you are driving around and having fun. Then something bit me. I really enjoyed it, and I realized I could make a living at it."

From building the first Funny Car from scratch and dropping in a Dave Zueschel–built 392 Chrysler (with Bynum handling the engine work), *Drag Racing* magazine broke down how all the remaining pieces came together:

Donovan equipment is used wherever possible and Milodon supports the lower end. On top is an Enderle injector under a 671 blower by Ronnie Hampshire, with an Engle cam in the middle of things. Cal Nelson furnished all the fuel lines, Airheart and Simpson are in charge of stopping the works at the end of the quarter.

Cragar wheels and a [TorqueFlite] typewriter transmission by Art Carr move the beautiful red metal-flake car that was painted by Gil's Auto Body. The body is fiberglass and all the aluminum work was done by Doug Kruse.

The Mustang chassis was built by Ronnie Scrima's Speed Products Engineering, and the body was from Cal Automotive.

Granatelli was onboard with continued STP sponsorship, an alliance that later proved critical to Murphy's move into the relatively new and controversial division. An altered-wheelbase category born of Super Stock, early Funny Cars were known in racing circles as "shake 'n bakes" due to their propensity for violent tire shake and unwanted flames.

Having a hot rod to go racing with, however, was only part of the equation. Whether disallowed due to safety concerns or simply to protect the macho vibe of the sport's most powerful and unpredictable division, multiple rules were put in place to keep women from competing in the sport's top-two divisions—Top Fuel and Funny Car. A 1967 *Hot Rod* magazine article entitled "The Female and the Fueler" captured the shifting cultural norms of the era, offering the subheading:

The "kitchen brigade" appears to have successfully jumped the gap from spectator to fuel car pilot. The pot's been bubblin' and has boiled itself down to the status presented here as we attempt to help you resolve: Should women drive fuel cars?

"I'm almost certain there has been some discussion over the possibility of some 'Imogene Glotz' getting stars in her eyes and creating serious problems from the mishandling of a very fast car," Murphy said in the article.

While male chauvinism certainly was not in short supply in the racing community, three-time NHRA Top Fuel champion Shirley Muldowney, whose drag racing adventures began on the streets of Schenectady, New York, was quick to point out that the other racers, for the most part, were not the problem.

"It usually wasn't the other drivers who had any issues with us," Muldowney added. "It was the hangers-on; star scratchers— I could use another word there, but I won't. You were much more likely to get a comment or a stare from some guy holding up a trailer for the weekend.

"'Jungle Jim' Lieberman actually was the first to come up to me and say, 'You drive like a man—you're good.' In my own mind, I knew I was decent. I knew I was getting the job done, but it came as a big surprise to some of the boys."

"Big Daddy" Don Garlits, who was ranked number one on the list of the NHRA's Top 50 Drivers list, was quick to point out Murphy's ability as well.

"Paula made it seem easy to drive a Funny Car; she was really comfortable in one," noted the Hall of Fame racer in an interview for the Paula Murphy biopic, *Undaunted*. "I just remember that she was good, she was good on the starting line; you know, she had good reflexes, and I don't remember ever seeing her get out of shape in the Funny Car."

Despite the early challenges for women trying to break into the sport, with the local paper noting they were "about as welcome in drag racing as [temperance crusader] Carrie Nation in a saloon," Murphy secured her Funny Car license, the first ever for a woman in a fuel class of any kind, with United States Drag Racers Association (UDRA) president Tom "The Mongoose" McEwen presiding over her licensing at Lions Drag Strip.

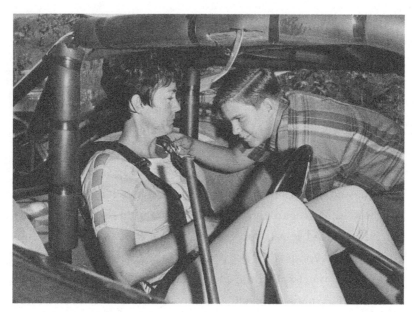

As a single mother, Paula Murphy often brought son Danny on the road when he was not in school, enlisting his help with the race cars, where he learned from mechanic Jack Bynum and others.
LandSpeed Productions Research Library / Paula Murphy Collection

"I first got my UDRA license, and then the AHRA [American Hot Rod Association] said they would be glad to have me, and I could run on their strips anytime," Murphy said in *Hot Rod* magazine. "Then I applied for an NHRA license, and after a meeting between some of the powers within the group, they decided they would go ahead and grant me a license."

Needing to complete twelve observed runs and undergo a "pilot's" physical fitness test, Murphy was licensed for a full year. "Licensing requirements were similar between all of the drag racing sanctioning bodies," said drag racing public relations icon Dave Densmore. "Obviously, the NHRA had the biggest stage then, as it does now, so it was beneficial from a business standpoint for the others to make it as easy as possible for the big names developed on the NHRA side to cross over."

Later in 1967, however, the NHRA pulled Murphy's license, as well as those of other women competing in the fuel classes, including Michigan's Della Woods, citing safety concerns and limiting the women to the lower-powered Super Stock division .

"They [NHRA] told us it's too dangerous for a woman to run an AA/FC," Woods said for DodgeGarage.com. "If a woman got hurt or killed, it would be bad for the NHRA's image."

The impact was immediate.

"I showed up with my brother, Bernie, to match race at Tri-City Dragway in Michigan and they threw me out of the track because the NHRA said it was too dangerous for women to have a fuel license," said Woods, the first woman in the five-second bracket in the Funny Car class, and the first woman to make it to a semifinal at an NHRA national event, an accomplishment that stood for twenty-two years. "All the big names were there that weekend, so it was really disappointing.

"They stopped us right at the gate," Woods continued. "My brother asked if we could at least drive through and turn around. Well, we drove in and stopped and started signing autographs. We thought, well, at least we'll get something done here.

"We were a real small—just the two of us—team, and we had to have that money," Woods said. "They finally came over and said we had to leave the track and they brought security over and we left the track."

With the Woods making anywhere between $450 to $600 in appearance fee money at the time, the loss of their Funny Car license forced them to race at outlaw tracks, facilities not sanctioned by any governing body.

"Losing the license was very tough for us," added Woods, who got her start at Motor City Dragway in New Baltimore, Michigan, in 1964. "We ran at Yellow River Dragstrip outside of Atlanta . . . there, they voted to not run against me, because if the Southern boys lost to me, it would look bad for them, and we were really running good then. So, they had me stand on the track, wave to the crowd, and run on my own."

Yellow River was later the site of a horrific crash that left eleven spectators dead and dozens of others injured. In a WSB Atlanta news report citing AHRA Director Rich Lynch, the drag racing organization labeled the facility "100 percent unsafe, especially in its lack of precautions for crowd safety."

Knowing outlaw tracks were a much more dangerous and less-than-welcoming place to move forward with her career and that Murphy had the influential Granatelli supporting her, Woods resorted to some long-distance leverage.

"I called the NHRA and said if you take my license, you'll have to take Paula's," Woods explained.

The ban impacted other female racers as well.

For Murphy, it wasn't as much about making a statement as it was simply about being able to continue to make a living doing what she loved and what she was good at.

"[The NHRA] pulled my license and Shirley Muldowney's and another girl who ran gas coupe, Barbara Hamilton [the first woman licensed by the NHRA to drive a supercharged car in competition with her blown '37 Willys gasser]," Murphy recalled for *Super Stock & Drag Illustrated*. "So, here the three of us were, with dates scheduled. Of course, Shirley had just a little car then, but I had a bunch of dates scheduled and I had to cancel them all at NHRA strips."

At one point, the NHRA had a separate women's driver's license," said Steve Gibbs, who managed Irwindale Dragstrip from 1966–68 and later became the NHRA Director of Competition. "That didn't last very long; they pushed the legal issues with it."

"Frankly, I played politics to get my license back," Murphy said in Pomona's *Progress Bulletin*. "I had to do everything up to and including the threat to sue the NHRA under terms of the 5th and 14th Amendments to the US Constitution."

Confident in Murphy's proven abilities and flexing the sponsor-ship muscle of STP, Granatelli also intervened and challenged the NHRA ruling. The result: "Miss STP"—and the Woods siblings—were back on the track and back in business.

While Murphy was not competing for NHRA points at the time, she did need to be licensed to participate at NHRA-sanctioned tracks around the country. Fewer available tracks meant less money for Murphy and less exposure for STP. Granatelli threatening to pull sponsorship money from the NHRA carried a lot of financial weight.

According to an article on NHRA.com following her passing in 2020, Hamilton endured two years and twenty failed petitions before getting her license back.

The fight to restore the right for women to compete at the highest levels of drag racing did, however, open the door for other women around the country at all levels, among them, Nellie Goins, who became the first African-American woman to find success behind the wheel of a Funny Car. Nicknamed "Nitro Nellie" after hitting 215 miles per hour piloting the family's Goins and Goins Conqueror injected nitro hot rod, Goins and her husband, Otis, ran their car basically out of their own pockets.

"No one ever mistreated us because of our race," she told NHRA.com. "In fact, we were pretty well ignored. We didn't have the big money or big sponsor, and we certainly didn't have time to socialize. We had a few fans, but because it was all busi-ness, nose to the grindstone to get the car ready, we didn't have time to chat with them. We didn't want them to think we were snobbish; we just didn't have time to talk to them. We were just trying to hold it together."

Several other women, many of them wives of drag racers or track operators, competed on strips in various classes around the country in the 1960s, among them Bonnie Anderson, Ginger Watson, Lucy Below, Bunny Burkett, Carol Cox, Dorothy Davis, Patty Young, Bernice Eckerman, Dorothy Fisher, Mary Ann Foss-Jackson,

Rose Marie Gennuso, Bettie Hendron, Shirley Shahan, and a host of others.

With drag racing promoters trying to increase overall interest in the sport, several all-women "powder puff" classes were added at various tracks, with Muldowney actually powering a 1963 Corvette to a powder puff championship before moving on to the top of the drag racing world as a three-time NHRA Top Fuel champion.

In 1971, promoter Tom "Smoker" Smith introduced Miss Universe of Drag Racing, a series highlighted by women competing for points. According to Niamh Frances Smith's *Raceway Hussy* blog, the first event in 1971 included eight entrants: Carol Henson with the Warlock Camaro, Carol Kile with her Family Affair Camaro, Fan Mellot with a Camaro dubbed Friends and Neighbours, Carol Wood in her Woods Wild Wheels Camaro, Jean Brown with the Rainbow Camaro, Nancy Wilson in a GTX and Burkett in a borrowed SuperBee. Henson took the win.

Going beyond local and regional match racing, Murphy and Muldowney scored national and international recognition, but never really squared off in meaningful races directly against each other. When they did, unfortunately one car or the other suffered some sort of mechanical failure.

At one point after they had their licenses pulled, Murphy suggested at dinner that Muldowney get a Funny Car, with an eye on getting several women to form a match-race attraction.

"Then she got Connie Kalitta's car and her career went from there," Murphy added.

"STP on Paula's car made all the difference in the world," said drag racing legend "Big Daddy" Don Garlits for a recently released documentary. "It actually got her in doors she couldn't have got into normally . . . between the STP logo and a woman driving the car, she could write her own ticket."

It wasn't quite "her own ticket," but there was certainly money to be made.

Paula Murphy was the first woman selected to participate in the NASCAR-sanctioned Union/Pure Oil Performance Trials, an event designed to help consumers make purchasing decisions with a selection of nearly seventy production vehicles.
LandSpeed Productions Research Library / Paula Murphy Collection

"Yes, you can make a pretty good living at it, but you spend an awful lot," Murphy said in a 1967 interview by *Moline Dispatch* columnist Paul Carlson. "[If] you are lucky and have a good year, I suppose it would be possible to gross $100,000 a year. But you'd spend $90,000."

As her drag racing continued, Murphy scored another first in 1968 when she was the first woman driver selected to participate in the Union/Pure Oil Performance Trials. Supervised and sanctioned by NASCAR, the trials compared braking, acceleration, and economy of more than seventy leading makes of 1968 American passenger cars, in an effort to help consumers make purchasing decisions.

Rules of the Road

The NASCAR Rules Committee set the "rules of the road" for the trials:

- All models were to be purchased with the standard engine.
- All cars were to have standard brakes (including linings) for that model.
- All cars were to have a standard tire size. Prior to the start of the trials, all entries were equipped with Union's Minute Man III tires. (Some entries, however, had special tire requirements to which the Minute Man III was not adaptable. These cars and others in its class were tested with original equipment tires.)
- All cars were to have standard axle ratio, automatic transmission, and such standard components as heater, radio, and seat belts. (Air conditioning was listed as required equipment in Class 1 through Class 4 cars.)
- All cars were officially entered by Union Oil company, however, manufacturers of the cars tested were invited to provide drivers and preparation crews for their cars. Manufacturer representation was limited to distinctly different models in each classification.

The Union/Pure Oil Performance Trials tested acceleration, braking, and economy across multiples classes of passenger cars. *Erik Arneson Collection*

As a late addition to the field at Riverside International Raceway outside of Los Angeles, and with no factory connections, Murphy, piloting a Pontiac GTO, finished second in Class 8, the Sports Intermediate class, behind the Chevelle SS 396, according to the *Los Angeles Times*. Other cars in Class 8 included a Buick GS 400, Dodge R/T, Ford Torino GT, Mercury Cyclone GT, Oldsmobile 442, and a Plymouth GTX.

Motorsports Hall of Fame of America 1991 inductee George Follmer, one of the most successful road racers of the 1970's, managed the Pontiac entries and selected Murphy as a teammate.

"You could see most of them watching Paula a little more closely," Follmer said in the *Los Angeles Times*. "But after a few days, you could see them [the men] drop their guard a little. They could see she knew what she was doing."

"This really was quite exciting," Murphy said in the same article. "And being the first and only gal in this really was a challenge. During the braking tests, for instance, I could see them [the men] all sitting there waiting for me to goof, but I didn't."

For the 1969 season, Murphy and Bynum briefly considered building out an attention-grabbing Cord before settling on a Plymouth Barracuda sponsored by Plymouth Dealers of Southern California and STP, a ride that logged 40,000 miles on tour that year.

"It was a Don Hardy 120-inch chassis originally built for Larry Reyes," Danny Murphy said. "It had the 392 Chrysler motor combination that came out of the Mustang (more or less). Larry had taken a job driving for Candies & Hughes and we were just around at the right time to buy it. That car was a good runner."

A good runner indeed. Murphy and Bynum's original Mustang Funny Car broke the 200-mph barrier in 1968, but the 'Cuda—with an Engle cam, Hedman headers, Enderle injectors, and Simpson parachutes—did it with regularity, the first time at the AHRA World Championships at Green Valley Raceway in Texas, where she delivered an elapsed time of 7.55 seconds.

"I'm an oddity, a rarity, and that helps," Murphy told *The Anniston Star.* "I have sixty to seventy bookings every year. But once I get the booking, then I have to run well. A drag strip hires me in and if I don't do a good job, they don't ask me back."

"I was very well accepted not only by the tracks but by my fellow racers," she added in *National Dragster.* "Back then, there was a lot of camaraderie between the teams helping one another out. We were a big family."

Often asked about her position on the growing "Women's Lib" movement of the late 1960s and 1970s, Murphy demurred in multiple interviews, "I was doing my own thing before those two words were ever uttered."

The move to a new hot rod, however, may have been less important than Murphy moving her racing operation back home to the familiar Cleveland area. Leasing a 30,000-plus-square-foot shop in the summer vacation community of Geneva-on-the-Lake, everyone came along for the ride, including Paula's father and her Alaskan Malamute, Kimo.

"It was a comfortable spot," Murphy said. "It was like going home. We rented a cute little house with two bedrooms and a basement . . . we had a good time there."

Danny would accompany the group and help during the summer racing season, returning in the fall to go to school in Southern California—where he sold STP stickers for a quarter.

Billed as "Ohio's First Summer Resort" and described by *Super Stock & Drag Illustrated* writer Alex Walordy as a "miniature Coney Island," Geneva-on-the-Lake bucked the growing trend of mega-parks, concentrating on simpler and less expensive outdoor activities. For some visitors to the Lake Erie community, a chance to see a collection of racers tuning their hot rods was one of them.

The shop, ironically christened "Fat Jack's Charm School" by racer Clare Sanders with a sign later hand-painted by nitro Funny

For Paula Murphy, her performance on the track had to meet or exceed the novelty of being one of the few women on the match-racing circuit: "I'm an oddity, a rarity, and that helps. I have sixty to seventy bookings every year. But once I get a booking, then I have to run well. A drag strip hires me in and if I don't do a good job, they don't ask me back." *Murphy Family Collection*

Car racer Tim Grose, became a bit of a tourist destination in its own right, with lines of onlookers trying to catch a peek at just what went into making rib-shaking horsepower.

"There was a tourist tram that ran the length of the town, and the turnaround spot for the tram was right next to the shop," said Grose, who at the time was working with Bryan Teal on the popular Super Chief hot rod, a ride he would later go on to drive. "There was a spray-painted sign originally, but I was a bit of a mechanical artist, and I spent a day lettering and painting a sign in a sixties style that marked the spot for the tourists."

"The shop was always open," Murphy said. "We never shut the big garage doors; the ventilation was bad enough. We would finish our work and start the car and the noise would attract people. When warm-up was complete, we would shut it off and run outside. It was always pretty 'fragrant' and the green haze and smell took a good while to leave the building. The people would often ask to go in to look at the cars. We said sure, but don't touch anything. They would head in and trot out crying."

"Fat Jack" was himself part of the attraction, his feats of strength noted by Walordy: "Where most people grunt while they put on hemi heads, and then struggle while they add on the headers, Jack preassembles a set of zoomies [header pipes] onto the hemi head, picks up the whole thing without any signs of strain, and snakes the zoomies between the engine and the chassis."

With plenty of space to sublease to other racers, or simply to serve as a stopover spot for teams passing through, the quiet

The infamous "Fat Jack's Charm School" in Geneva-on-the-Lake, a small resort town on Lake Erie where Murphy and Bynum set up shop for the match-racing season. *Paula Murphy Collection*

community garage became home to some of the sport's hot shots, producing a cacophony of sounds that drew curious locals and tourists alike.

"A lot of teams would come by and stayed because finding a place to stay in Geneva wasn't easy," Murphy said. "So, they could find a place to stay and share our shop."

Nelson Carter's familiar Dodge Charger Super Chief, with Bryan Teal and later Grose at the wheel, and the Frank Huff-Clare Sanders Camaro were season-long neighbors in the shop, with others coming and going. Among them were Tom McCourry and his wife, Lynda. Tom was campaigning the four-engine Riviera WagonMaster, which was the former Tommy Ivo Showboat dragster before McCourry added the aluminum wagon body crafted by Tom Hanna.

"There was a guy named Hank, who owned the shop [and] a bunch of nearby bungalows and would rent them out by the day, the week, or the month," Grose said.

"It was a wonderful little town, and Paula and Jack were obviously well known there," said McCourry's wife, Lynda. "We usually had a new place to be every week during the summer racing season, but when we had the time, we would use their garage as a kind of base and stay at a local hotel.

"Paula was really respected in the drag racing community," Lynda McCourry added. "She wore a lot of hats back then as a mother and a homemaker, a drag racer and just keeping her profession going. When we'd hang out with them, Jack could be a little intimidating, so I'd stay quiet as a church mouse, but it was a lot of fun. It was a real adventure and we met a lot of interesting people."

"When I met Paula, I didn't know that much about her," Grose said. "But we had a great synergy. We were able to talk about things other than racing, so I got to learn about the person Paula was, not related to racing.

"From day one, I always admired her greatly," Grose added. "She was so unassuming. If you didn't know what she did for a living, at a grocery store or anywhere she went, you would have assumed she was one of the locals—and yet, look at how connected she was and how much she already had accomplished."

According to a December 1971 issue of *Super Stock & Drag Illustrated*, Jim Nicholl's latest rear-engine rail, Huff's Super Vega, and Warren Gunter's Durachrome Bug also made appearances at the Charm School. Drag racers of the era often personified the "work hard, play hard" mantra, with a small, oval go-kart track surrounded by tire stacks serving as the local playground.

"On a fairly regular basis, some of the other traveling hoodlums would show up in town and converge on the go-kart track," Danny Murphy said. "It wasn't a few kids running around in circles. It was a bunch of drag racers and their crews out there trying to kill each other . . . a couple of them went over the tire barrier and ended up outside.

"We'd have 'All-Star' races after hours and the track owner would adjust the governors to allow for more speed," Danny Murphy added. "It was serious racing."

Paula added with a sly chuckle, "We eventually got banned from the track."

"There were regular poker and Chinese Checkers games going on—anything you could bet on," Danny Murphy added.

In the evening, Paula often retreated to her rental home or shopped in nearby Amish country to stock the rental house, but many of the visiting racers found their way to The Castaway, a tiki-styled dinner club just outside the village of Geneva-on-the-Lake on Route 534, offering everything from its signature bikini-clad "Go Go shower dancers," women who danced to music inside a working shower that was rolled out onto the stage, to live music from notable artists, including country giant Conway Twitty.

Entry to The Castaway was through the mouth of a huge Easter Island Moai that had gas flames coming out of its eyes.

At the time, Ohio was still serving three-two (3.2) beer, beer with 3.2 percent alcohol or less, so some of the younger members of the group could join in the fun.

"You could drink at eighteen, or if you looked eighteen," Danny Murphy said.

Lake Erie comfort and nostalgia aside, there was a hugely practical reason for setting up racing operations in the Midwest.

"It was a good central headquarters; it was perfect," Paula Murphy said. "It was close to the interstate, and we'd run Indiana, Illinois, Wisconsin, Michigan, Pennsylvania, New York, and a bunch of other places."

From the West Coast to the East Coast, the action crossed from California strips like Lions Drag Strip, Irwindale Raceway, Orange County, and Carlsbad raceways, to busy Midwest tracks like Great Lakes Dragaway, US 30 Drag Strip, and West Salem, Ohio's, Dragway 42.

Scoring gigs on the East Coast, Bynum and the Murphys frequently raced at the always-busy Atco Dragway, a quarter-mile track in New Jersey that opened on Memorial Day, 1960. Atco was less than an hour from Philadelphia, so they also made stops at Niagara Drag Strip, Maryland's Capitol Raceway, and many others.

With Murphy doing the driving and Bynum handling the tuning, Paula's son, Danny, was the lone crewman during his summer break from school.

But when Danny was back in California, Bynum, known to pinch pennies, would higher local kids who lived near the garage to help out with the work on the car, including a youngster who lived just across the street from the garage named Patrick Gallagher.

"Instead of a rooster crowing in the morning, Jack would be up early and holler at the top of his lungs, 'Gallagher, get your fucking ass out of bed,' and ten minutes later, the kid would be running out of his door and headed to the shop," said Grose. "I'm sure the daily routine woke up more than just the kid."

"I did a lot of tearing down and putting things back together," explained Danny, who spent a lot of time with Gallagher fishing and hanging out at The Castaway when they were finished working for the day. "I did a lot of the under-engine work at the races. I'd pull the pan, pull the bearings and re-torque everything underneath the motor. I helped drive a lot to and from the races. I was the guy sitting in the car for warm-ups and on the ride back from the top end . . . whatever needed to be done, including cleaning the car and polishing the aluminum."

"Most of the time, we were racing over the weekend," he added. "A Friday or Saturday night and maybe a Sunday. A normal busy week, we'd race a couple of times a week, although we did have at least one time when we ran five times in a ten-day period (that was the most). That was nightmarish."

"At one event, we spent an entire night at the drag strip," Danny continued. "Everybody else had gone home, and the track operator left some lights on for us and we rebuilt an engine right there in the parking lot and put the car back together. We started the damn thing around five o'clock in the morning, loaded it up on the trailer, and took off for the next stop."

Usually returning to Ohio on a Monday, they'd tear everything down and make any needed repairs before putting it all back together, hopefully in time to load it back on the trailer by Thursday evening or Friday morning.

"When we'd get to the track, we'd unload the car and get it cleaned back up again," Danny said. "Jack would get busy mixing fuel; Mom would pack her parachutes and sign autographs . . . once we were fueled up and ready to go, we'd drag it up to the starting line. Jack would be out in front of the car. I was behind the car and after Mom did her burnouts, I'd motion to Jack where the tire marks were, so we could back the car up in her tracks.

"If you could get away with not hurting anything on a match race weekend, you did good," Danny added. "Sometimes, we could go a couple of months, and other times we could blow up two motors in a weekend. The work never ended."

Cut from the same mold as nomads, according to drag racing icon Don Schumacher, the real moneymakers mapped distances between tracks, highlighting their next stage by tracks within 600 miles or twelve hours.

"We'd be gone more than two hundred days a year," said Schumacher. "But we made a really good living."

"'Fat Jack' certainly was a key partner to Paula through all of it," Schumacher added. "He looked after her safety in the race car, around the track, and going down the road."

With her West Coast credentials and STP profile, Murphy was commanding $1,000 an appearance if she completed three runs, and the Midwest tracks offered the most opportunity.

"I didn't run a whole lot of NHRA races, mainly because the NHRA didn't pay me to show up," Murphy said. "The AHRA and IHRA [International Hot Rod Association] both paid me appearance fees. We had to run three runs to get paid the full amount and most of the time we did. We made about three appearances a week . . . that's the way I made my living."

Muldowney, who often scheduled match races on Wednesday nights, Saturday nights, and Sunday afternoons, with a 500-mile drive between Saturday and Sunday events not uncommon, offered another challenge racers occasionally met at smaller tracks— getting paid.

"If it rained, we didn't make anything but a $500 rain-out guarantee—*if* we could get the promoter to keep their word," Muldowney said. "Most of them did. Some didn't. One even came up to me years later and said, 'Remember when you kicked my wife's ass out of the bus down in Lakeland, Florida?' Yep, I sure do. I remember it well. Connie [Kalitta] and I were both

An attention-grabber in the driveway and a strong runner in
1969, the Plymouth Dealer's "Miss STP" Barracuda with a Don
Hardy chassis and 392 Chrysler Hemi regularly topped 200 mph.
LandSpeed Productions Research Library / Paula Murphy Collection

there trying to get our money. [The promoter] was being hard to
deal with that day.

"We finally got it, but the wife came in and stuck her nose where
it didn't belong and turned around and headed for the door of the
bus and my foot was right behind her," Muldowney said. "I had my
days when I had to hang in there, and I had to be strong at times
or I would have gotten walked on like an old show and I would not
have made the grade."

Promoters also occasionally tried to dock racers money for red-
lighting or not going fast enough.

"There were places I went back and raced again and again and
again, and there were some places that I raced one time and that was
it for reasons of my own," Muldowney explained. The emphasis on

nationwide match racing may have been, at the very least, inspired by Bynum's pal, "TV Tommy" Ivo, recognized as drag racing's first professional, as the actor-turned-racer was the first to travel the country making a living with his attention-grabbing four-engine dragster.

"The big sponsors had not yet come into drag racing," said Ivo, who made the decision to go racing full time following the end of his twenty-four-episode stint as Heywood Botts on the 1961–62 television sitcom, *Margie*. "STP took care of Paula at some level and provided a lot of promotion for her, but our bread and butter came from match racing."

"You couldn't afford to go out and run these national events one after the other," Ivo said. "And it wasn't even one after the other in those days. When I first started, there wasn't even one national event until 1955, and others were slowly added in over time."

Like Prudhomme, Ivo and Bynum were part of the Los Angeles car culture in the 1950s, meeting regularly at the iconic Bob's Big Boy in Burbank near Toluca Lake, where the red-jacket-and-white-pants Road Kings car club, including the likes of "The Snake" and Ken Stafford, talked hot rods and street racing with dozens of local racers.

Ivo's bold move quickly became the talk of the Los Angeles drag racing community, a move with which Bynum was familiar.

"I was the first one to ever go out [in 1960] and make my living from drag racing," Ivo said. "Don Garlits did some traveling on or slightly before that, but he'd go out for a weekend and go up to North Carolina and run a race and go back home to his regular speed shop in Florida.

"I was the 'first professional' is what they say, and Paula followed along doing the same thing," Ivo added. "That's where we made our money."

Both were popular attractions, with Ivo even sending out film clips from his movies and television shows to local news affiliates,

Murphy with one of her early "Miss STP" match-racing Plymouth Funny Cars. *LandSpeed Productions Research Library / Paula Murphy Collection*

promoting the movie-star drag racer coming to town. Ivo blazed the match-racing path for Murphy, Bynum, and others to follow.

"They had a couple of tracks here in Los Angeles and a couple more around in California, but with the population back East, the drag strips were built on top of each other," Ivo explained. "I ran eight races in one week one time—I ran a Sunday afternoon at Atco and a Sunday night up at Englishtown, but of course we weren't running the cars as hard as they are nowadays."

Twice Ivo and his crew of two ran one hundred match races in a single season. "Over a thirty-year period, we towed enough to go to the moon and back three times," Ivo said. "We ran the wheels off those things, and I was everything from the shop sweeper to the CEO. More people came out to check out the movie star than the race, but we helped expose a lot of people to drag racing . . . when they saw the fire and brimstone and found out they could drive their own personal car down the track, they were hooked. Ultimately, that was my contribution to the sport."

Often running into each other at match races across the country, Ivo, Murphy, and Bynum would catch a movie together after a day of racing. But on one occasion, Murphy would miss an evening at the theater. While waterskiing on a Wisconsin lake near Great Lakes Dragaway in Union Grove, Ivo attempted to dump his pal Bynum, who was at the end of the ski rope.

"I whipped the wheel and Paula fell across the boat and bumped her leg," Ivo explained. "We were going to go to the movies that night, and she said, 'Well, my leg's kind of hurting me, I think I'll stay home.' When we came home, she was sitting there in a cast."

Despite the accident, the group enjoyed spending time together whenever they crossed paths on the race circuit.

"Paula is a classy lady—she's the apple of my eye," said Ivo, who inducted Murphy into Don Garlits's International Drag Racing Hall of Fame in 1992. "She and my wife, Inez, were very good friends as well."

And while Murphy and Bynum were a perfect pair at the drag strip, the couple was never linked off the track.

"I was never romantically interested in Jack," Murphy said in a 1989 *Super Stock & Drag Illustrated* article. "Though I think he was with me. He is a dear man and I really appreciate what he did, but he was not the type of man I would have considered marrying. He was my buddy."

For Danny Murphy, the relationship with Bynum was complicated. Danny was missing a father figure for most of his young life, and Bynum was "pretty rough and tough and heavy on the kid" according to Paula.

"We definitely had a love-hate relationship," Danny explained. "At the end of the day, I loved the guy. He taught me a whole lot, but he was definitely a taskmaster and he made me mad quite often. I really liked what I was doing and most of the time, we got along well enough and we had a lot of good times.

"Any street sense that I have today, all came from Jack," Danny added "My grandfather taught me a lot about being a good person, but Jack taught me about street sense, and that's more than my real father ever did for me."

With his grandfather setting the work-ethic example, Danny looked to Bynum and others from the racing world, including Frank Huszar from Race Car Specialties (RCS), but it was Paula who provided as much stability as possible.

"She was a good mom in that she always tried to include me in things," Danny said. "Especially when I was younger, before pro racing. My father disappeared when I [was] young and didn't provide much, if any, help. She worked hard to put a roof over our heads. I got to travel on occasion and see some of the country with her. She was very much a regular mom in every way except her love of cars."

Paula and team load an STP car onto a trailer in 1970. *LandSpeed Productions Research Library / Paula Murphy Collection*

Danny added, "I have to admit, it was cool being part of that, traveling all over the country and getting to know many of the great racers."

In 1970, Paula, Jack, and Danny were back with a Plymouth Duster body and a tow vehicle provided by Jack Prince, a Los Angeles Chrysler/Plymouth dealer. The emphasis on racing across the Midwest, however, cost the team its sponsorship from the overall LA dealership group. Racing mostly in the Midwest simply wasn't selling cars in California. She did, however, win the Olympics of Drag Racing at Union Grove and the New Jersey State Drag Racing Championship at Atco Dragway.

Off the Strip

That same year, Murphy left the quarter mile briefly to compete in the Mint 400, the oldest and most prestigious off-road race in America. A far cry from straight and flat, the bone-jarring endurance race is run in the foothills of Las Vegas and is known as "The Great American Off-Road Race."

Murphy teamed with fellow Grenada Hills racer and car owner, Janet Elliott, in a buggy with a Bandido chassis and Corvair power. Once she tried off-road racing, she was hooked. Murphy spent the rest of the decade racing in the Mint 400, Mexican 1,000, and Baja 500.

She took on yet another racing surface just for fun when she entered the 1970 $50,000 Kings Castle Grand Prix snowmobile race in North Lake Tahoe. She joined a VIP entry list that included Parnelli Jones, Bobby Unser, Roger Ward, Don Drysdale, John Brodie, Deacon Jones, Joe Louis, Ken Venturi, Bob Rosburg, Lee Marvin, Evel Knievel, and Mama Cass.

"Let me tell you," Murphy told *The San Francisco Examiner* following the event. "Riding one of these things on a course like that isn't as easy as it looks."

"This thing," she added, brushing some snow off the polished top of the snow mobile, "actually tossed me when we were going about forty-five miles per hour. I've done a lot of racing in my day, but I've never fallen out of any of my cars."

This spirit of adventure went on to define much of Murphy's record-setting career—climbing into wildly diverse vehicles, charging across a variety of terrains, testing herself every bit as much as the machine.

A smiling and clean Murphy before one of her numerous off-road adventures. *Petersen Automotive Museum*

Chapter 4

NASCAR Stars and Rocket Cars
(1971-1975)

"Like bats from hell, these $20,000 machines flash down the quarter-mile asphalt strip in less than seven seconds at speeds of more than 200 mph. From design to destination of light traps down the asphalt line, Funny Cars are a high-octane trip into another racing dimension."
—*Mike Barry,* Quad-City Times, *1971*

Racing from small-town drag strip to even-smaller-town drag strip and back again, it was Murphy's well-tested versatility that made her a standout in the world of motor sports. And it was the early 1970s, just before the country's first major gas shortage sent the nation into panic, that best captured her elite adaptability and confidence behind the wheel.

Piloting everything from a desert-racing equipped Volkswagen to a 1,500-horsepower quarter-mile Funny Car to NASCAR star Fred Lorenzen's STP-sponsored Pontiac, Murphy continued to demonstrate her competence, competitiveness, and willingness to try new things at the track—any track, any surface, any time. Murphy teamed with Tom Cox to race the 1971 Baja 500 in June— an off-road event started in 1969 on the Baja California Peninsula that began in Ensenada, wound through the Baja California Sur and back up the Peninsula. Murphy was behind the wheel of the race-prepared Beetle. The pair finished third in their class (L500), citing a missed path coming out of a dry lake as the reason for not finishing higher.

"There are just so many paths to choose from," Murphy told *The Decatur Daily Review*. Finishing the race in just under 16.5 hours, Murphy attested to the challenge of her latest adventure.

"Yes, the Baja is as rough as they say, but not as bad as the Mint 400," Murphy continued. "[There] is no trouble keeping awake during the night . . . tired or not, the jolts won't let you sleep. Besides, it takes both pairs of eyes to keep you on-course."

Always on proper message for the media and her sponsors during her decades-long career, Murphy admitted recently that the off-road experiences were not among her favorite for multiple reasons.

"I didn't like it at all," Murphy said from her Southern California home. "First of all, one of the last ones I went on was in an Olds Cutlass [1972 Mexican 1,000 with co-driver Jack Mendenhall]. We didn't even have a spare tire, and, of course, what did we lose, we lost a tire. We lost the whole bloody wheel . . . it went bouncing off into the tundra."

"Here we are stuck out there in 'nowheresville' in the middle of the night," Murphy continued. "Finally, somebody came to our rescue, and I spent the night sleeping in the back of a pickup truck . . . an open pickup truck."

But the escape from the desert was far from over.

"Friends of mine, Deke Houlgate and his wife, got me a ride with a retired TWA pilot who had a little rinky dink one- or two-engine little plane, a little puddle jumper that came in and got me," Murphy added. "We're flying around, and the pilot says, 'It's getting dark and we can't fly across the border at night.' We stopped at a fishing camp along the border and, of course, he wanted to hit on me. I was so mad. I would've shot him if I'd had a gun and I probably would have gotten away with it. We eventually resolved that issue and he finally flew me out and got me home."

"I swore that was the last time I was going to do such a stupid thing . . . going out in that stupid desert," Murphy said. "You get lost, even in the Mint. You're driving at night with great big huge headlights, with other competitors sabotaging the course, moving markers around along the way. It was an awful sport. You got really dirty and your body really takes a pounding."

Murphy did, however, take on a few additional desert races, including the 1973 Mint 400. She teamed up with Mendenhall in the Pea Soup Ford pickup, built by Bill Stroppe and named for Vince "Pea Soup" Evans, patron of racers and owner of the Pea Soup Andersen's restaurant in Buellton, California. The truck had been driven a year earlier in the Mint by movie and television star James Garner.

Paying the Bills

Despite exploring other racing opportunities, it was drag racing that paid the bills. Immediately following her 1971 Baja run, Murphy flew to Illinois, joining Bynum and Danny at Motion Raceway outside of Assumption, Illinois—a strip that operated from 1970 to 1983. Murphy was part of a lineup that included her pal Della Woods's Funny Honey Dodge Challenger, Butch Maas and his Hawaiian mini-Charger, Arnie "The Farmer" Beswick's Boss Bird Pontiac Firebird, Frank Oglesby's Quarterhorse and Larry Fullerton's Trojan Horse—both Ford Mustangs, Tom

The Pea Soup Andersen's Special, the Olds Cutlass piloted by Jack Mendenhall and Murphy in the 1972 Mexican 1000. The ride lost a wheel during the race, leading to an overnight stay in the back of a pickup truck before Murphy was flown home.
LandSpeed Productions Research Library / Paula Murphy Collection

Hoover's White Bear Dodge, and "Big Mike" Burkhardt, piloting a Chevy Camaro.

Campaigning an STP Special Duster hardtop powered by a 392-cubic-inch, supercharged, fuel-injected Chrysler Hemi with more than 1,500 horsepower, Murphy picked up where she left off, with *Super Stock & Drag Illustrated* breaking down the powerplant in the new ride:

"Bynum and Danny Murphy have used a lot of resourcefulness in building the 392 Chryslers that power Paula's racer. Howard rods and Forged True pistons make up the bottom end, with Engle Cam, Donovan 2-inch valves and rockers, Gary Dyer blower, Enderle injection system and Cirello magneto, treated on the parting edges with sealing wax to detect cap removal. The Milodon girdle and lubrication system keep the moving parts stable, while the zoomie headers apply sufficient downforce on the front for Bynum to have removed 40 pounds of front ballast."

Coming into the race, Maas's hot rod, tuned by legendary crew chief Roland Leong, had won the 1970 and 1971 NHRA Winternationals with a top speed of 215.76 miles per hour. On her second run, however, it was Murphy who set a track speed record at Motion, hitting 211.76 mph before losing a blower during her final pass.

"She was one hell of a race car driver," said Linda Vaughn, who was a mega-popular fixture at drag races around the country where she represented Hurst and other brands. "I really liked the way Paula carried herself. I liked 'Fat Jack' and he adored her. He looked after her. She wasn't like the other women in racing. She had class. She didn't swear or show her ass. She was a lady and a woman and a hell of a race driver. I respected Paula right off the bat.

"Jack was kind and considerate, but rough around the edges and I liked that," added Vaughn, who was inducted into the Motorsports Hall of Fame in 2019. "He was a tough boy, and he worked his ass off for her . . . and Paula drove her ass off for him. I thought they made a hell of a pair, and I was so in love with both of them."

In the midst of the busy match-racing season, the marketing mind of Andy Granatelli found yet another way to elevate "Miss STP" into the spotlight while at the same time selling a lot of product and supersizing STP brand awareness. Leveraging the growing popularity of NASCAR, Granatelli set Murphy up in Fred Lorenzen's STP-sponsored Plymouth in an attempt to set a women's closed-course record on the country's largest and fastest stock car track—Alabama International Motor Speedway, now Talladega Superspeedway.

Lorenzen was not just any stock car driver. Nicknamed "Golden Boy" and "Fearless Freddie," he won twenty-six times in NASCAR's Golden Era of the 1960s, including the 1965 Daytona 500. Lorenzen later was named one of NASCAR's 50 Greatest Drivers,

Sponsored by Plymouth Dealers of Southern California, "Miss STP" barnstormed a variety of drag strips across the country, including Atco Dragway in New Jersey, an active strip since 1960.
Erik Arneson Collection

entering the Motorsports Hall of Fame in 2001 and the NASCAR Hall of Fame in 2015. In 1963, he became the first NASCAR driver to earn more than $100,000 in a season.

The 1971 season was a bit of a comeback attempt for Lorenzen, who took over behind the wheel of the No. 99 Plymouth owned by Ray Nichels and Paul Goldsmith. Well, for a few hours one afternoon, Lorenzen's ride belonged to Murphy, and she made the most of it. On a billboard in Daytona, Murphy had seen that racer Vicki Wood had hit an average speed of 147.42 mph at the 1959 Century Run in Daytona Beach, upping it to 147.928 in 1962. Now she wanted to break that record.

"We feel confident that she will set the record," STP publicist Bill Dredge told the *Advertiser.* "It's just a question of how fast she will go."

Murphy prepares to go for the women's closed-course record at Talladega. *NASCAR Archives & Research Center*

Mission Accomplished

In the December 1971 edition of *Stock Car Racing* magazine, positioned next to ads for Iskenderian Racing Cams, quick-change gears, and Weiand "Hi-Ram" manifolds, Murphy offered a first-person, six-lap account entitled *My Ride at Talladega*:

> Well, I thought it was a little too late to back out now. Here goes, and I yanked the steering wheel to the right and started climbing up onto the track between the first and second turns. Before I knew it, though, I was moving down the backstretch already—and I'd been running slow!
>
> Three or four laps got the car up to speed and settled me down. I began turning laps in the high 140-mph range. Once

I began to get acquainted with the car, I really started to enjoy myself. I ran about 35 laps during the first session.

But I have to admit to one goof—a dandy that sent the racers running for cover. Despite my efforts to be calm, I actually was pretty keyed-up when I left the pits to start the actual record run, for I gave the engine too much gas as I let the clutch out and the result was that I looked like I was trying to do one of my drag racing burn-outs. Then the car's rear wheels got completely loose and the back end started (to get) out of control. The nose headed for the concrete pit wall. All I could see outside the car were a lot of male racer-types heading for the infield as quick as they could. I corrected the wheel to the right and shot over toward the grassy strip and let off the gas for an instant. Although it seemed like an eternity and that there wasn't going to be any STP Oil Treatment Special in the race two days later, I finally got things sorted out and was on my way onto the track. The worst was over. I hoped.

As I mentioned, after one warm-up lap, I decided I better get the run over with. So, I got on the gas to take up where I left off in practice—a notch over 169 mph.

My arms and shoulders were sore since I overdid the first session in the biggest and heaviest race car I'd ever driven, and I could see where I wasn't going to be able to crank that thing through the turns all day, anyhow. I did about four laps, all over 170 mph, and the best one of NASCAR timer Joe Epton's clocks was 171.499 for the new women's mark for a closed course.

I must admit that I'm pretty satisfied with the way things went during this project, all except for my foolish-looking little slip getting out of the pits to begin the run, but I'm pretty certain that if the schedule had permitted the green flag to stay out for me for just a few more laps, I could have got my courage up and knocked out another mile-per-hour or two for the record. I'd like to go back just as soon as possible, and try again . . .

Murphy's official average speed of 170.499 mph on August 20 secured the record by a wide margin and would have qualified her for thirty-third on the grid for Sunday's Talladega 500. Lorenzen then drove the Pontiac to a fourth-place finish in Sunday's race before using radio communication to formalize a long-rumored split with STP and Granatelli, citing performance issues.

NASCAR founder Bill France congratulates Murphy after she set a closed-course record for women of 170.499 mph at Alabama International Motor Speedway, now Talladega Superspeedway. Murphy was behind the wheel of NASCAR Hall of Famer Fred Lorenzen's STP-sponsored Plymouth for the effort. *NASCAR Archives & Research Center*

1972

In 1972, Murphy returned to the match-racing circuit behind the wheel of a flame-painted Plymouth Duster. The November issue of *Super Stock & Drag Illustrated* broke down some of the inner workings of the hot rod, noting Romeo Palamides and Tom Daniel had done the aluminum work and that the early 392 hemi was running at a full 424 cubic inches "by virtue of a .030 overbore and a .250 stroker crank with Mildon main caps."

The rest of the package according to the magazine: Venolia 6.5:1 pistons and rings, Howard rods, and an Engle 169 cam and kit with Donovan rockers and stock valves. Valley Head Service heads, Enderle injection, Cragar drive and manifold, Dyer 6-71 blower at 24 percent overdrive, Cirello mag ignition at 34 inches, Autolite AG401 plugs, Hedman headers, Milodon oil system, Crowerglide triple-disc slider, and STP filters with balancing by Valley Head and machine work by Bud Richter.

The 1972 season also saw Murphy return to the Mint 400 in March with Jack Mendenhall and his Olds Cutlass. The 1972 entry, originally built by Vic Hickey of Ventura, California, was owned by Garner, who had co-driven it to a second-place overall finish in the Mint just two years earlier.

The schedule and the variety of racing disciplines never slowed. Just a week later, Murphy, named one of four outstanding women athletes by managing editors at The Associated Press, competed in the IHRA World Record Drag Race Championships at Charlotte Motor Speedway. She competed as part of the Plymouth manufacturers team with Don Schumacher and was billed in advertisements to race on Sunday against some of the biggest names in the sport, including the legendary Mickey Thompson (who pulled out due to injury and was replaced in his Ford entry by Dale Pulde), Tom Hoover (Dodge), Wayne Mahaffey (Chevy), and Jungle Jim Lieberman.

Touted as "one of the biggest two-day meets in drag racing history," the races were run on Charlotte's one-eighth-mile strip.

Unfortunately, Murphy's hot rod broke during a first-round burn-out, unceremoniously ending her day.

Then came the rocket car.

In the Fall of 1972, Murphy returned to the Bonneville Salt Flats for what appeared to be the next exciting chapter in her life of speed and firsts behind the wheel. This time she was introduced to the Pollution Packer rocket car, designed by Bloomington, Minnesota's, Ky "Rocketman" Michaelson and funded by the Minneapolis businessman Tony Fox. The car was named for one of Fox's multiple business interests—a trash compactor, and flew under the Tony Team, Inc., banner.

Murphy prepares to take her turn behind the wheel of the rocket-powered Pollution Packer at the Bonneville Salt Flats. *LandSpeed Productions Research Library / Paula Murphy Collection*

Murphy, comfortable in the otherworldly setting of the Bonneville salt, was intrigued by the opportunity and the who's who list of Bonneville legends accompanying the effort, including record-setters Craig Breedlove and Art Arfons.

According to DragList.com writer Franklin Ratliff, the Pollution Packer was created when Michaelson mounted the motor from the Reaction Dynamics X-1 in his Top Gas dragster chassis. The Pollution Packer had a fuel tank larger than the X-1's but still mounted vertically behind the cockpit. Unlike the X-1, the two fiberglass-wound spherical nitrogen bottles were behind the fuel tank, stacked one on top of the other. The fuel system was pressurized to over 500 PSI—75 PSI more than in the X-1—thus raising thrust from 2,500 pounds to about 3,000 pounds.

The Pollution Packer made its public debut on Labor Day 1972 at Union Grove, Wisconsin, with runs of 6.13 seconds at 248 mph and 5.68 seconds at 280 mph. The car was stealing the show on the match-racing circuit, first with Michaelson behind the wheel, but later with Top Fuel journeyman Dave Anderson.

But Fox, always on the hustle, was looking to draw attention on a larger stage, a national stage. Described in an NHRA.com article as "an enterprising and cunning carny barker of a businessman who not only owned [a] snowmobile company but also had delved into every-thing from weight-loss equipment to trash compactors," Fox was a Minnesota neighbor of Michaelson, and the pair set their sights on a series of publicity-driven world record attempts on the salt.

Looking much like a conventional dragster, Pollution Packer hit the salt at a mere 750 pounds. According to an article in *Performance Cars* magazine, the hot rod was powered by an "unusual rocket engine" that weighed 57 pounds and consumed 16 gallons of 98 percent hydrogen peroxide, which was fed into the engine while under intense pressure. Dick Keller, the chief engineer for Gary Gabelich's Blue Flame rocket car, the world record holder at the time, was the rocket engineer for the Pollution Packer.

According to the magazine: The fuel decomposes and expands when forced through a silver catalytic screen; the end product spews out of the tail in a combination of super-heated steam and oxygen gas, which, by the way, is absent of any pollutants. Pressure was 550 pounds per square inch in the fuel tank with about 3,600 pounds of thrust (3,000 horsepower). Piloted by Anderson, Michaelson's childhood pal from Minnesota, the racer pushed the Pollution Packer to twelve national and world records at Bonneville.

Of note, with no records on the SCCA books for jet or rocket cars from a standing start, each faster run secured a new acceleration mark, with Murphy later noting, "It was like being shot out of a gun."

When Murphy got her turn in the cutting-edge hot rod, she scored yet another historic feat, becoming the first woman ever to drive a rocket-powered racing car. With Fox hosting an audience, providing catered meals and even music from "a Hawaiian rock band," the car was set at lower power settings than those used for Anderson, in part to provide a higher level of safety for a woman driver, and less conspicuously, so she didn't run faster than Anderson.

Murphy ran a 90-percent hydrogen peroxide mixture, while Anderson ran at 98 percent.

Murphy, however, promptly established the women's world record from a standing start for the quarter mile. She flashed through the two-way quarter miler at more than 250 mph, with each pass being the quickest in history at 6.60 and 6.70 seconds.

"It's so much safer than a Funny Car," Murphy told writer Jack Scagnetti. "I can't believe it. There are no pistons to break, no danger of an oil bath, no possibility of fire. The engine is behind you and the car drives straight as an arrow. I love it!"

According to Ratliff, after acceptance of hydrogen peroxide rocket dragsters by NHRA, the Pollution Packer became the first car to clock over 300 mph at an NHRA National event during the Gatornationals on March 18, 1973.

During the 1973 NHRA Springnationals, the Pollution Packer became the first four-second dragster of any kind when Anderson clocked a pass of 4.99 seconds at 322 mph. At the 1973 US Nationals at Indianapolis, Anderson attained his best performance with a pass of 4.62 seconds at 344 mph.

Making Her Mark

As the Women's Lib movement picked up steam in 1973, marked by the Billie Jean King versus Bobby Riggs televised "Battle of the Sexes" tennis tournament that drew a record-setting US audience of 50 million viewers and a worldwide audience of 90 million viewers, interest was growing in the ongoing social changes and what they meant for sports. With King winning the match handily, 6-2, 6-1

Tony Fox's Pollution Packer trash compactor was a sponsor on the 1972 Mexican 1000 ride, a product label that later marked a dramatic turn in Murphy's career. *LandSpeed Productions Research Library / Paula Murphy Collection*

in the Houston Astrodome, the "anything you can do, I can do better" battle was on. But Murphy, who often distanced herself from the movement, had been living by the motto since birth.

That growing curiosity was not limited to the United States. Murphy and Bynum took their hot rod across the pond later in 1973, joining a list of racers who had been invited to compete at Santa Pod Raceway in Podington, England. A former World War II air base, Santa Pod opened as Britain's first permanent drag racing facility on Easter Sunday in 1966. Run by Bob Phelps and his son, Roy, the two focused on bringing some of the best American drag racers to their venue. Roy began to visit the bigger events in the US, where he spent time working the pits, looking for those who were willing to make the journey and earn a few dollars.

Big-name racers, including Don Garlits, Gene Snow, Raymond Beadle, Sammy Miller, Al Segrini, and Darrell Gwynn, all made the trip over the years, with the intent of putting on an exhibition and selling their equipment into the European market before returning home.

"The technology and the cars were so far behind over there, so they were always hungry for access to our equipment," said Gwynn, whose life-altering accident happened during an exhibition run at Santa Pod in 1990. "They thought it was the greatest thing since sliced bread to have American drag racers at their track. They always made us feel very welcome . . . and they were definitely there to see *you*."

In 1973, Murphy joined a group that included up-and-comer Don Schumacher and the go-to man for international drag racing, Tony Nancy, with two scheduled appearances at Santa Pod and another at the HMS Daedalus naval air station.

"That last Duster was a completely new car, chassis and all," Danny Murphy said. "Romeo Palamides built the chassis on that thing—he basically built the whole car. The body was by Ron Pellegrini. It was the same body [as the previous car] but more modern with dragster style roll cage. We added a 392 Chrysler and later with the Ed Pink motor, it was a rocket ship."

Schumacher, a 2019 Motorsports Hall of Fame of America inductee, noted that being with the more experienced racers was important to his development, especially in an unfamiliar, albeit welcoming, setting.

"Paula and Jack already had been racing for several years, so having them to lean on during that trip was a real benefit to me," said Schumacher, who piloted his popular Stardust Funny Car. "I felt like Robin Hood over there . . . from the reception we received at the track to the way we were treated at the hotels.

"I'd get in the car to do a burnout and the cheering was so loud, I could hear it in the car," Schumacher added. "That had never happened at any track in the United States. That was a real high point in my career up to that point."

Unfortunately, the events were a bit of a washout with Schumacher noting, "The cars came over in pieces and sat out in the rain. It was really challenging to get set up for a solid run."

The all-concrete track could be unforgiving as well.

"In my first run—at the top end of the track, there is quite a bad bump, and I hit that bump very hard and poked a hole in my oil pan," Murphy said from the Santa Pod pits in a videotaped interview later posted on Bangshift.com. "So, we had to have that welded and repaired [in time to make the second-day passes at Santa Pod]. Today, I took it a little easier than I did yesterday."

Following the exhibition runs, Murphy and Bynum sold the car to Owen Haywards, who rechristened the flopper Houndog 7, part of British Drag Racing Hall of Fame member Nobby Hill's legendary Houndog line of entries.

Returning to the US, Michaelson came calling again with another opportunity to get behind the wheel of the newly redone Pollution Packer. This time he had set his sights on Sears Point Raceway, which was snuggled in the rolling hills of Sonoma, California's, wine

Murphy traveled with Don Schumacher and others in 1973 to England for exhibition runs at Santa Pod Raceway and the HMS Daedalus naval air station. *LandSpeed Productions Research Library / Paula Murphy Collection*

country. Michaelson had split from Fox and Keller and made some modifications to the original design. For Murphy's ride, the ever-present "Miss STP" label was back on full display.

"I finished my season back east and sold my car in England, went back to California and then up to Sears Point, where the first race with the new car was planned—a WCS [NHRA World Championship Series] event," Murphy told *Super Stock & Drag Illustrated*.

The goal for the day was to make two passes, one at 270 mph and a second at 280 mph, besting her record of 258 mph. "This is the first time we've run this car 'at speed,'" Murphy noted in the *Santa Rosa Press Democrat*. I'm going to try for a record run on the first pass."

Businessman Tony Fox turned Murphy's and driver Dave
Anderson's 1972 land-speed record attempts at the Bonneville
Salt Flats into a spectacle, bringing in an audience, providing
food, and hiring a band. *LandSpeed Productions Research Library /
Paula Murphy Collection*

She explained her confidence in operating cars at high speeds.
"I worked into it gradually and know what to expect," she added in
the *Press Democrat*. "I know what to expect."

Murphy wrapped the interview with a bit of an ominous statement: "If I should die, I would know I had a good life and got to do
more in a car than any other woman. It's been a pretty good life."

The sentiment nearly proved prophetic.

On her very first pass, Murphy's long run of racing luck simply
ran out. Long known in motorsports circles, the maxim understood
by all is, "It's not *if* you will crash, it's *when*." Her friend, Linda
Vaughn, had an eerie premonition leading up to the run; "women's
intuition" as she described it.

"I didn't want to really tell her how I felt," Vaughn said. "I didn't
want to put it in her head because I respected her, but I had already
seen a dragster blow up at Gainesville and I had been the guest of

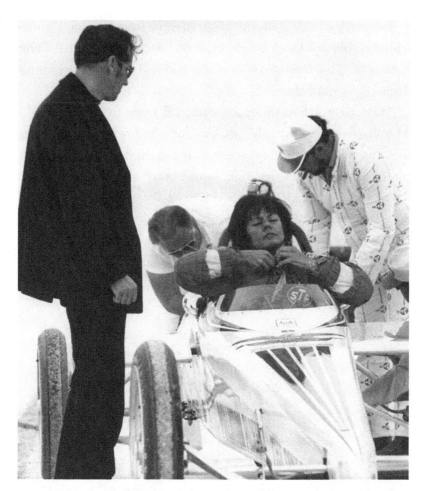

Speed merchant Art Arfons, half brother of Walt Arfons, whose jet car Murphy piloted to a Bonneville speed record years earlier, looks on as Murphy prepares for a run in the Pollution Packer rocket car. *LandSpeed Productions Research Library / Paula Murphy Collection*

generals at several rocket tests where they admitted rockets were really unpredictable.

"I said, 'Paula, you don't have to prove yourself to anybody,'" Vaughn continued. "'You're a great driver, but you never know what a rocket is doing to do.'"

Despite Vaughn's concern, and even more from her son, Danny, Murphy strapped in. A couple of years later, she would tell Polly Rayner of *The Morning Call* that she had had her own disturbing dream the night before.

"The night before the race I dreamed I was in a fiery crash," Murphy recalled. "It really shook me up . . . I never had a dream like this before in all my years of racing. I felt it was some sort of omen. But on the practical side, I talked myself into believing that it was all psychological. I was driving a brand-new car and was quite concerned about all the things that could go wrong. With all these worries on my mind, I decided it all came out as a bad dream."

But the next day, that dream became a scary and painful reality. Bee Laurence of the *Napa Valley Register* captured the near-tragic moments:

A who's who on hand as the Pollution Packer set thirteen national and international speed records at the Bonneville Salt Flats. From left, Gary Gabelich, Art Arfons, Doug Rose, Craig Breedlove, Roger Gustin, Dave Anderson, Joe Petrali, Paula Murphy, Tony Fox, and John Paxson. *LandSpeed Productions Research Library / Paula Murphy Collection*

The car is long and lean, a swathe of STP red on the Sears Point Raceway. It gurgles quietly as the driver, hidden behind mask and goggles, applies the throttle. A wh-o-o-o-s-h of steam spurts from the rear, a signal to the crew that the car is ready. The men push it to the starting line. Staging lights flash through a series of yellows, then green—and a tremendous, ear-blasting roar splits the air as the car takes off, a blur of color streaking down the track.

The new rocket dragster, in its debut at Sears Point Sunday, is traveling 254 official miles per hour when it reaches the end of the measured quarter mile. The driver releases twin parachutes to slow the speed. The power system should shut off automatically, allowing the car to coast to a stop.

Something is wrong.

Something Was Very Wrong

"The parachute mountings failed and off I went," Murphy explained from her California home. "When I hit the parachutes, the tabs ripped off and the parachutes went south, and I just kept on accelerating. I went up a hill—they judged I was seventy feet in the air before I came down. Fortunately, I rolled the car and didn't do endos [end-over-end summersaults] in it."

Adding in the *Super Stock & Drag Illustrated* article: "It was the first full pass I made, and everything kept running and running—and I went off the end of the strip at probably 300 mph. I thought 'this was it'; I knew I was dead. I was knocked out, and when I came to, we were upright and everyone was running around the car, saying, 'Get out of the car, there's a fire.' I said, 'No, my suit isn't burning; I've got to sit here and compose myself.'"

While able to climb out of the car, Murphy suffered fractures of her third and fifth cervical vertebrae, spending time in Marin General Hospital before moving to a Los Angeles hospital closer to home.

"It was a horrendous experience," Murphy continued. "I broke my neck, and I was in a cast for months and then a brace. Sitting all strapped in, you stretch, or you flop about, and that is what did it. There wasn't much clearance between my helmet and the roll cage, and I had this big mark on my helmet. . . . If it had been any other drag strip, I probably would have been killed because of running into railroad tracks or houses, or off a cliff or whatever. But at Sears Point, it's big rolling hills. There was a fourteen-foot-wide gate in the fence, and I was fortunate enough to aim through it, though at the time, I didn't have any idea of what I was doing. I don't care what anybody says, when you have a tremendous crash like that, it takes a lot out of you."

Depressed for some time after the crash, Murphy wasn't sure what the future held for her.

Murphy's second time behind the wheel of a newly rebuilt rocket car virtually ended her high-speed racing days, as the car failed to come to a stop, ran off course, and flew into the air in Sonoma, California, leaving Murphy alive but seriously injured. *LandSpeed Productions Research Library / Paula Murphy Collection*

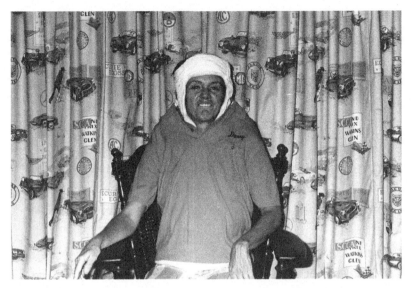

Following the rocket-car accident at Sears Point Raceway, Murphy was in a cast from her head to her hips for months, suffering fractures to her third and fifth cervical vertebrae.
LandSpeed Productions Research Library / Paula Murphy Collection

"I would burst into tears when someone just looked at me," Murphy told *The Morning Call*. "What was I going to do with myself."

"I was supposed to be in the [body cast] for six to eight months," Murphy added in the *Escondido Times-Advocate*. "But I talked the doctor into taking it off early. I wore a brace instead."

"It fused but it wasn't straight," Murphy added. They said if I was to slip and fall I could be seriously injured or paralyzed. But you can't go around padded for the rest of your life. Besides, I love racing."

Originally, planning to get back in a rebuilt rocket car after recovering from the injury, Murphy opted out, saying in the interview, "No, I can't get back into that thing."

In a cast from her head to her hips in the beginning, the healing process took about four months, moving from the cast to a brace along the way. Murphy continued to work, however, honoring car show appearances and other commitments in her cumbersome and uncomfortable condition.

Sadly, in March of the following year, Anderson was killed driving Michaelson's rocket car at the IHRA Southern Nationals at Charlotte Motor Speedway. He was thirty-six years old.

According to *Competition Plus*:

> The stories have varied throughout the years regarding the cause of the crash. Unofficially, race officials from the era testified the team over-fueled the car, while other accounts blame a parachute failure, brake malfunction, and possibly a chassis failure.
>
> The rocket cars had no fuel shut-off and essentially a driver was along for the ride. For Anderson, the ride was a wild one. The parachute deployed but failed to open, trailing the rocket as it careened through the short shutdown area. The dragster went into a spin and struck down two crewmen on a dragster parked in the area before they could get out of the way.
>
> The car collided with several wreckers parked in the shutdown area and broke in half when it struck the six-foot wall that shielded the main grandstand from the racetrack. Both crewmen reportedly died upon impact and Anderson, according to newspaper reports, died en route to the hospital. . . .
>
> Less than a year earlier, Anderson had become the first to break the five second mark on a quarter-mile track, at 4.99 seconds, and a top speed at the finish line of 322 mph.

The Charlotte deaths marked the end of a deadly five-year span from 1970 to 1974 that resulted in sixty-two fatal drag racing crashes according to a list cited in *MotorTrend* magazine.

"[The rocket cars] did a lot of damage," said one-time NHRA Director of Competition Steve Gibbs. "We lost quite a few guys to them damn things. I never really cared for them that much . . . Paula was lucky to survive her crash at Sears Point.

"Tony Fox was the one who kind of talked the NHRA into allowing the rocket cars to run," Gibbs added. "After Dave Anderson in Charlotte, we had the incident in 1975 where Russell Mendez was killed in a rocket car in Gainesville . . . they were dangerous. They just went too fast and were too light."

For Murphy, racing would never again be about record-breaking speeds, certainly not rocket car speed. The remainder of her drag racing career would be behind the wheel of less powerful and more predictable rides.

The helmet Murphy was wearing during her crash behind the wheel of the ill-fated rocket car is on display as part of the Paula Murphy collection in the Motorsports Hall of Fame of America in Daytona Beach, Florida. *Erik Arneson Collection*

A Royal Adventure in Monte Carlo

While recovering from the rocket car crash, Murphy accepted an invitation from French oil maker, Elf, to participate in an all-women road race—the fifteen-lap Renault 5 Ladies' Monte Carlo Grand Prix—in conjunction with the 1975 Monaco Grand Prix on the same circuit used for the Formula One race. Murphy was the only American driver in the twelve-car field.

The race was won from the pole by Marie-Claude Beaumont, a driver for Ecurie Elf Ladies' team for the European rounds of the World Sportscar Championship in 1975.

Murphy's experience on the racecourse was much less memorable than the evening before, where she was invited to attend a cocktail and dinner reception with Prince Rainier and Princess Grace of Monaco.

She recounted the experience for *Stock Car Racing* magazine in 1976:

> I open this envelope and it's this beautiful engraved invitation from Princess Grace and Prince Rainier. I'm at a disadvantage, not being able to speak the language so I ask the man at the desk to read this to me. He said, "Well, it's a cocktail party, and long dress is required, and it said RSVP," and I said, "How do you RSVP, particularly when its only three hours before party time?" And he said, "I'll take care of it," and he called and told them.
>
> I get in the room, and the bag isn't even unpacked, and I have to shower and wash my hair and get everything together. I get the dress out, and I can't find the dumb shoes I had packed for the dress. And all I have are my Indian moccasins that I wear racing and these yellow shoes I had on last night. Then I couldn't find the evening bag. So, what do I have but a yellow attaché case type thing that I carry my passport and all the junk, my daytime bag and my $2 Mexican macramé

Murphy's invitation to the palace reception and dinner that was
held prior to racing in the fifteen-lap Renault 5 Ladies' Monte
Carlo Grand Prix, in conjunction with the 1975 Monaco Grand Prix.
Paula Murphy Collection

over-the-shoulder stringed purse. I thought, "I can't go in
there holding my car keys in one hand and my Kleenex and
matches in the other."

I wore the yellow shoes. I thought, "I can't go barefoot,
and if I walk pigeon-toed maybe no one would notice." So,
I got in my little car that's all painted up with my name and
the American flag, and there could be no question who I was
and that I was there for the race. I took my invitation with me
into the parking area, and I get out of the car and we go to
this fabulous archway. There's all these guards standing there
with their guns and their swords.

All these people are walking in with ermines and minks
and gorgeous dresses, and here I am sneaking into this place.
I follow the crowd up this long hallway, and there's this beautiful room with gold ceilings and Oriental rugs, the reception

room, and of course, Princess Grace. She looks like $9 million, beautiful, very gracious. And she appeared very glad to see me. And then I met her husband and daughter, and I don't know who-all else, and I'm looking around, and everybody is speaking French. I don't know a soul in the place.

So, I kind of walk around the fringe of the room, and I'm gawking, and finally I sit down in a chair, and there's Aristotle Onassis sitting on the couch with three women talking away. I almost went over and introduced myself, because he is the only one I knew. The butler came over with a big silver tray. So, I had a Champagne and smoked a cigarette.

The dress I have on has narrow straps that button in the back, and then a little bolero jacket that ties in the front. I look down and the strap has come unbuttoned on the dress and is hanging out the front of my bolero. So, here I am trying gracefully to tuck this thing back up in there, and I didn't see any ladies room on the way in, and I couldn't ask anybody could you button my dress back here for me, and I really felt like a bump on a log.

I thought, well, I've had my glass of Champagne, and I've met them all, I was supposed to meet someone here, but he didn't show up yet—that was going to be my excuse if somebody said something. I was going back to my hotel to find him. Nobody understood anything I said. But this man got the picture that I was going to leave. So, he escorted me down the next flight of stairs, and everyone snaps to attention, and I went to my car.

After some confusion with security in her attempt to leave, it was the next day before Murphy realized her mistake.

"The next day, I pull into the pit area, and there's Jackie Stewart waving me down," Murphy recalled in the article. "So, I stopped, and he got into the car and introduced himself like I didn't know him and said Princess Grace was worried about you last night, and she wanted to know what happened to you. Well, I thought it was a cocktail party—at least that's what the man at the hotel desk had interpreted to me—and it turned out it was a dinner, and I had left before dinner."

On the track, things didn't go much better.

"I was running really good," Murphy recalled. "We practiced at some track way out in the boonies, and I was running pretty good. The car seemed to be OK. On race day, I lost a gear—it was either second or third gear. Well, you can't run, particularly a tight little course like that without all your proper gears. So, I parked it. I thought it was better than finishing dead last. I took the DNF.

"I was kind of glad to get out of there," she concluded.

Johnnie Parsons and Paula Murphy in front of the Taj Mahal. The trip was monitored and recorded by the United States Auto Club (USAC). *LandSpeed Productions Research Library / Paula Murphy Collection*

Chapter 5

Around the World
in a Pontiac Sunbird

"It's really useful to travel, if you want to see new things."
—*Jules Verne,* Around the World in Eighty Days

aving spent the previous decade or so driving farther "to" races than "in" races, Murphy scored a unique opportunity to change that recurrent dynamic as part of America's ongoing 1976 bicentennial celebration. An opportunity she referred to as, "A once in a lifetime experience."

Minneapolis-based National Car Rental, at the time operating in more than sixty different countries across three affiliated brands—National, Tilden, and Europcar—charged its public relations agency, Padilla & Speer, also based in Minneapolis, with finding a unique way to promote the company's international reach.

With America still recovering from the ongoing pain and national division sustained as a result of the Vietnam War, the worldwide celebration of America's two hundredth birthday looked to be the red-white-and-blue party to end all parties. Padilla & Speer leaned into the oversized mixture of patriotism and propaganda in a huge way, creating the first-ever US Bicentennial Global Record Run. The PR firm sent out a press release titled, "'Snow White' Murphy Accompanies Six Men on Global Record Run," highlighting the tone of the era. But Murphy rolled with it in the release, renaming it, "Snow White and the Six Dwarfs," stating, "Hope that doesn't offend any of them, but I don't think it will. We've learned to get along pretty well, and they take plenty of cheap shots at me."

The race, which consisted of driving across five continents, twenty-nine countries, and more than twenty-five thousand miles of road of all sorts of terrain, would feature two drivers: thirty-nine-year-old Murphy and 1950 Indianapolis 500 winner Johnnie Parsons, then fifty-eight, who was handpicked by longtime racing pal and USAC Director of Competitions Henry Banks.

Mapping out the route was no easy feat. Obviously impacted by geography, the itinerary also faced a few political challenges and multiple changes, including an early plan to include part of the Sahara Desert in the journey—a plan that ultimately was voted down due to logistics issues. Yugoslavia ended up being the only Communist country on the itinerary. As National Rental Car President Joe W. James told the *Star-Ledger*: "To get clearances for travel in most Communist countries would be beyond our capabilities. Besides National doesn't have any operations in Russia or China."

The plan was ambitious. The result was epic. A June 1976 article in the *Newark Star-Ledger* reported that each driver would be paid $150 per day plus expenses. The trip took ten months to plan and would cost nearly $200,000, a figure that undoubtedly ran over, as the planned sixty- to seventy-day trip ended up taking 102 days, according to a July 8, 1976, article in the New Orleans *Times-Picayune*.

National Car Rental and Pontiac, one of its fleet providers, split the bill. National wanted to show off its around-the-world availability, while Pontiac aimed to highlight the durability of two of its 1977 models. Parsons piloted the new 5-liter (301 CID) V8 1977 Grand Prix, rated by the EPA at 16 miles per gallon city and 23 mpg highway. Murphy got behind the wheel of Pontiac's new 2.5-liter (151 CID) Iron Duke powered four-cylinder 1977 Sunbird, not yet available to the public, with 19 mpg city, 25 mpg highway ratings.

The Iron Duke was Pontiac's answer to the 1973 oil crisis, with a team of Pontiac engineers eventually developing the 151-cubic-inch, straight four-piston power plant into a race engine. Labeled "unkillable" later by *Driving Line,* the Duke served Murphy and the team well, going on to power a wide variety of vehicles in the decades to come.

"The big issue after [1973] was fuel economy," said Ed McLean, a Pontiac district sales manager at the time in Charlotte, North Carolina. "We had the Iron Duke, which we actually made into a race engine later in the 1980s. We went drag racing with it. We went GTU racing."

Fittingly, the trip started on the Fourth of July, with Parsons departing from Minneapolis and Murphy from Daytona Beach, Florida—where she followed NASCAR pace car driver Enoch Staley on a parade lap to open the Firecracker 400 at the iconic Daytona International Speedway. In her rearview mirror—the front row of A. J. Foyt and Cale Yarborough, followed closely by Richard Petty and Bobby Allison. A little farther back in the field was Janet Guthrie, another female racing pioneer, who finished the race fifteenth after starting from the thirty-third position.

Murphy and Parsons met in New Orleans, joined by retired Pontiac assistant chief engineer Ed Windeler; driver/mechanic Steve Mignone, who piloted the support van loaded with spare parts; official USAC observer/recorder Donald Davidson; cinematographer John Mueller; and Padilla & Speer VP and crew coordinator Tom Lee.

USAC, which had worked with National on several other tests already, often was enlisted for third-party verification by companies looking to give their products more credibility with consumers— the automotive version of the *Good Housekeeping* Seal of Approval.

Murphy began the US Bicentennial Global Record Run at the start/finish line at Daytona International Speedway in Daytona Beach, Florida. *NASCAR Archives & Research Center*

Murphy's Daytona Beach sendoff began on Friday, July 2, at the Holiday Inn Surfside's Tides Hall, where Medal of Honor recipients were being honored. After she was pointed out at the event by race announcer Chris Economaki, Murphy told the crowd about the upcoming trip. Barbara Taylor of the *Daytona Beach News-Journal* later wrote about what she said.

"No one has ever achieved this goal before," Murphy noted in the *Daytona Beach News-Journal*. "I've had my firsts in my racing days, but none that will match this one. I've driven everything from stockers to drags to rocket cars. This race certainly will be different."

Murphy noted the climate changes expected along the way ranged from desert heat to monsoons to snowstorms, with the crew prepared for all conditions—they even sent snow tires ahead for the trek up the Andes. But Murphy, who raced on the salt at Bonneville in the 1960s and through the desert in the 1970 Mint 400, had little concern with the unpredictable driving surfaces. Her history of driving hundreds of miles at a time and towing a vehicle to the next match race had prepared her well for the effort.

"I'm not even thinking of what the roughest part of the haul will be," Murphy told the *Palm Beach Post*. "I love to drive, so there's no fear of a long trip like this spooking me. I'll probably want to drive our local highways the day after I get back."

According to the July 8, 1976, article in the *Times-Picayune*, Parsons was confident, but aware of the challenges—including the 17,000-foot Andes mountains and a 200-mile unpaved stretch of the Alaska-Canada Highway. He also considered the trip to be about more than just a drive around the world. "We're going to try to spread some goodwill," Parsons said in an article in the *Ville Platte Gazette*. "Too many unpleasant things are happening, and this is just the contrary."

From New Orleans, the pair crossed into Mexico via Laredo, Texas, on July 9, where they were greeted by a ceremonial police escort, which delivered them to Mexico City. Once there, Murphy and Parsons presented their first US Bicentennial token to Manuel Aguilar Inzunza, Director General of Foreign Offices in the Secretariat of Tourism. Since the trip had been sanctioned by the US Bicentennial Commission, this would be the first of many similar presentations Murphy and Parsons would make as they traveled the world. The State Department had input on the international itinerary and provided the Bicentennial medals that were to be passed out to foreign dignitaries along the way.

The Adventure Begins

The next few legs of their global journey were documented by the *USAC News*:

> The crew left Mexico City on Monday for Guatemala City, 800 miles south, passing out U.S. Bicentennial lapel pins, paper weights, lighters, ball point pens and other items carrying the Global Record Run symbol. Heavy rains in southern Mexico delayed their departure from the capital city until Monday and they arrived in Guatemala City on Wednesday. Vehicles were reportedly sliding off roadways in southern Mexico, so the layover was a wise one. Guatemala City is celebrating their own bicentennial, having been founded in 1776 to serve as the country's capital after an earthquake damaged an earlier capital.
>
> The next stop was San Salvador, El Salvador, where they encountered a traffic problem. It seems that one of the police motorcycles escorting them out of town was involved in an accident with a car, seriously damaging the motorcycle, not the rider. After a short delay to render first aid, they proceeded eastward on the Pan American Highway toward the Honduras border, then to the Honduras capital city, Tegucigalpa, a charming city nested in a mountain valley.

Most stops included public relations initiatives, from lunches to speaking engagements to photo ops with the local dignitaries at signature landmarks.

The path through Panama included the quite-deadly Darién Gap jungle, the sixty-six-mile connection between the North and South American continents labeled the "world's most dangerous journey." Undrivable, the team traveled by boat to their next stop in their quest, where they were delayed for a few days while banana shipments took priority.

Parsons remarked about the treacherous mountain driving: "It's no Sunday drive." He said he was going to buy a pair of leather gloves for better control.

They reached San Jose, Costa Rica on July 18 and resumed their drive the next morning, headed for Panama City, some 500 miles south.

From Mexico City southward, the crew experienced less and less motorized traffic and more and more pedestrian and animal road-blockers. At times, they had to blow their horn to bull their way through herds of oxen and cows being driven down the highway by vaqueros (cowboys). Paula Murphy explained: "Everything they say about driving at night in Central America is true." She continued: "My advice is DON'T DO IT." In small towns, the roadways are used for social gathering places as well as walkways for those who don't own cars.

Border crossings were involved in Honduras and Nicaragua with a Nicaragua customs officer sealing the trunk on the Grand Prix (where the record run souvenirs were kept) with express orders to remove the seal only at the Costa Rica border.

Murphy and company drew a crowd at every stop along the way. Working in coordination with the US State Department, the effort was sanctioned by the US Bicentennial Commission. *LandSpeed Productions Research Library / Paula Murphy Collection*

"We were going to call it 'Around the World in 80 Days,' and instead we called it 'Around the World in 80 Delays,'" Murphy said for a 1989 article in *Super Stock & Drag Illustrated*. "We were hung up with a lot of stuff, which was kind of fun in a lot of places."

Farther south, the group was keenly aware of the volatility around changing world events as they traveled through Santiago, Chile. The bullet-riddled road signs they passed along the way served as visible reminders that just three years earlier, a military coup d'état, including an attack on the presidential palace, La Moneda, deposed President Salvador Allende.

Once in South America, the drive continued through Ecuador, Peru, Chile, Argentina, Uruguay, Paraguay, and Brazil, with a brief delay in Argentina after being pulled over and charged with driving with their dome light on at night . . . they were trying to read a map.

According to *USAC News,* the South American expedition had taken them through pre-Incan ruins in Peru, across the formidable Andes mountains, through politically tense Argentina, and into Uruguay, where they viewed the spectacularly beautiful Iguazú Falls, and on to Rio.

The *Ville Platte Gazette* reported the final portion of the Pan American leg of the Global Record Run ended in Rio de Janeiro. The cars' bumpers were removed so the vehicles would fit into the cargo space, where they were lashed onto special air freight pallets for their flight across the Atlantic to Casablanca, Morocco, with a stop in Dakar, Senegal, for fuel.

Aside from the 350 miles from Panama City to Buenaventura and a 100-mile ferry trip from Buenos Aires to Montevideo, the team covered more than 11,000 miles (nearly one third of the trip) by road.

Through Central and South America, Murphy recalls a question asked more than once by various hotel clerks: "Seis hombres, una mujer?"

"What was it like to drive around the world with six men? I loved it," Murphy said in the *Ville Platte Gazette.* "I'm used to competing in a man's sport—racing. I was comfortable and so were the fellows."

Northern Africa, Europe, the Middle East, and Asia

After the 4,400-mile flight from Rio de Janeiro to Casablanca, Morocco—where Murphy and Parsons plunked down $8 apiece for camel rides—they were off to Tangier and then Spain. When the group reached Paris on August 31, Murphy commented that the Champs-Élysées, the central boulevard in Paris, "would make a great drag strip." From Paris, they traveled to Munich, West Germany; Austria; Venice, Italy; Greece; Belgrade, Serbia; Yugoslavia; Istanbul and Ankara, Turkey; Iran; Pakistan; and Bombay, India.

In Parsons's memoir, *Never Looking Back*, he noted that on the drive from Pakistan to India, they didn't drive after sundown, as "people living in the desert would come up and sleep on the shoulders of the road, the blacktop continuing to hold the heat far into an otherwise chilly night."

Once they reached Bombay, Murphy and the team stopped briefly to ride an elephant. "We were driving along and there was a big elephant on the side of the rode with a sign that said something like, 'Get your photo taken here.' I said we've got to stop and do that, and we all got to ride an elephant." Murphy commented that India was a "place completely different than we had ever seen."

"One day, we were driving along, and I looked over, and here going down the road was an old man on a bicycle," Murphy recalled. "He was completely naked with a long, flowing white beard and a

Parsons and Murphy taking a boat trip down the Seine as they pass by the Louvre art museum. France was the sixteenth country to be visited by the two drivers. *LandSpeed Productions Research Library / Paula Murphy Collection*

large turban on his head . . . he was just peddling along completely naked. I thought to myself, 'Well, now I've seen everything.'"

Bombay marked the end of the longest segment of the trip, and the group faced a little bit of an optics and credibility dilemma as they considered the rest of the journey. The original itinerary had them flying to Japan, but part of the group thought flying west to the United States and, ultimately, Anchorage, Alaska, to complete the final legs of the trip would be the easiest and least expensive way to proceed. However, the winning sentiment was focused on the journey being an "around the world" trip, so continuing east was the correct path to finishing that challenge.

Catching a different kind of ride in India, Murphy noted: "We've got to stop and do that, and we all got to ride an elephant." *LandSpeed Productions Research Library / Paula Murphy Collection*

Almost Home

On September 29, another airlift carried cars and crew from Bombay to Tokyo, Japan. The remaining legs took them through Anchorage, Alaska; Los Angeles; Las Vegas; and Denver before Parsons returned to Minneapolis and Murphy to Daytona Beach.

"You miss a lot (about America)," Murphy noted for the *San Francisco Examiner* as the entourage re-entered the US.

"Yeah, like salad dressing, cheeseburgers, and cold pasteurized milk. Some countries have no beef," Parsons interjected.

From Alaska, the final challenge was the ALCAN (Alaska-Canada) Highway, 1,500-plus miles of dusty, gravel road with very few paved surfaces, initially built as a military supply route during World War II. When it rained, the cars spent large stretches sliding around in the mud.

Logistics and Statistics

USAC tracked a wide range of statistical information along the way, including, but not limited to, gas consumed, average driving speed, mileage between stops, and weather and surface conditions (with maintenance checks noted). Gas prices ranged from 17 cents per gallon in Iran to $2 per gallon in Western Turkey.

"We kept track of everything," Murphy noted in Louisiana's *Ville Platte Gazette*. "We logged start and stop times to the second, miles traveled, average speeds, gas mileage—the works. All the data was meticulously recorded by Donald Davidson, an observer/statistician from the United States Auto Club (USAC). The 110 pages of USAC data and a few thousand photos thoroughly documented our trip."

Times (due to different starting and finishing points)

Murphy: 105 days, 2 hours, 29 minutes, and 25 seconds

Parsons: 102 days, 18 hours, 26 minutes, and 54.7 seconds

Her official odometer reading upon completion: 26,402.3 miles

The group enjoyed a police escort in Vancouver as it approached the US border crossing in Blaine, Washington.

On October 15, Parsons rolled into the Minnesota State Fairgrounds to take his checkered flag, and a couple of days later, Murphy took a victory lap around Daytona International Speedway to complete her journey.

The only real mechanical mishap happened outside of the Twin cities just miles from the finish, when the support van driven by Steve Mignone lost a wheel.

Murphy, who witnessed plenty of "political strife and economic tragedy" summed up the experience in a story for United Press International (UPI): "This may sound corny, but you don't realize how glad you are to be an American until you return home.

"I missed a lot of racing while we were gone," Murphy added. "I'm heading to Florida to pick up my race car."

In 1976, Murphy and 1950 Indianapolis 500 winner Johnnie Parsons spent more than one hundred days driving "around the world" in a pair of Pontiacs as part of a National Rental Car publicity tour—the US Bicentennial Global Record Run. *LandSpeed Productions Research Library / Paula Murphy Collection*

Bumps in the Road and
Asking for Directions

Through it all and despite "tropical storms in Panama, monsoons in Bombay, and traffic jams in Paris," the Pontiacs driven by Murphy and Parsons experienced no major mechanical issues outside of reactions to poor quality gasoline along the way.

But that didn't mean there were no challenges.

At one point, Parsons had to jump off a ferry to help push it off of a monsoon-soaked riverbank in India. Gas shortages in Turkey had the group nervous about their next fill-up, but once they crossed into oil-rich Iran, fuel was cheap—eighteen cents a gallon—and plentiful.

In lighter moments, there still wasn't much room to let down your guard. Being ever-alert was mandatory. "You can't ever relax," Murphy said in the British Columbia *Province* six weeks into the journey. "You have to be ready any second for a chuck hole in the middle of a clear stretch. You must be ready to swerve any second to avoid a pedestrian, bicyclist, horse, ox, goat . . . you name it. I damn near hit a pig up in Mexico, and that really would have messed things up. Don't get me wrong," she added. "Much of the road has been good, and I'd have gone in a buckboard if that had been the deal. But you have to watch what you're doing every second."

To pass the time while driving, Murphy often had whomever was riding with her read local travel guides out loud so she could learn about the city or country they were driving through. During at least part of the trip, she had the co-pilot read James Michener's popular novel, *Centennial*.

Murphy also noted that she had one of the most important functions on the otherwise all-male team. "I was always the one who would have to ask for directions," Murphy said with a chuckle. "Not one of those guys would ever open their mouth. God forbid a man should ask for directions."

The trip became affectionately known as "Around the World in 80 Delays," but the crew finally made it home. For Murphy, the official odometer reading at the end of the adventure—26,402.3 miles in a Pontiac Sunbird. *LandSpeed Productions Research Library / Paula Murphy Collection*

A Glimpse into the
US Bicentennial Global Record Run

Each of the members of the team experienced the adventure in their own way, but it was Tom Lee who took the time to record some of his personal observations. His notes, which appeared in the *Omaha World Herald*'s Sunday magazine, provided an unfiltered glimpse into the group's travels. The PR executive was familiar with South America, having spent a year in San Paulo on a US Agency for International Development project, according to *USAC News*. Lee's poignant remembrances, published nearly a year after the trip, painted quite a memorable picture:

- Noticing nose prints on your windshields, and remembering they were left that day by a mob of smiling, waving kids at a Chilean gas station. Those nose prints would reappear all around the world, with the laughter and the smiles and the "Hello, Americans."
- Feeling as though you are tiptoeing into Turkey under a black shroud of fear and uncertainty spun by hundreds of "experts" who have never been there . . .
- Being held at machine gunpoint by 12 youthful, terror-eyed Argentine soldiers after you made a mistake and crossed through a military control checkpoint near the Chilean border without stopping. You're hoping all your North American friends will think you've kept this incident in perspective and will not cast aspersions on your Latin American friends.
- Being disappointed that Casablanca was neither dark nor mysterious and delighted to experience what appeared to be intrigue and mystery during dark Arabian nights in the tiny communities of the Middle East and Asia.
- Flying over the DMZ in Southeast Asia at midnight on an Air India flight from Bombay to Tokyo and recalling that

Making many stops to take in the various cultures, the team consisted of just seven people—Murphy; Parsons; retired Pontiac assistant chief engineer Ed Windeler; driver/mechanic Steve Mignone, who piloted the support van loaded with spare parts; official USAC observer/recorder Donald Davidson; cinematographer John Mueller; and Padilla & Speer VP and crew coordinator Tom Lee. *LandSpeed Productions Research Library / Paula Murphy Collection*

this is one of the few times since you left home July 4 that you've had time to think about Vietnam; wondering what life is like in that battle-scarred region beneath your plane.

- Remembering people, like your first escort into a foreign country ... Raul Maliay Lardnan, an angel from the Mexican Department of Tourism. Raul led you through northern Mexico, stopping first to show you his church in Nuevo Laredo with its 400-year-old statues. You watched him cross himself self-consciously, and you now recall variations of this religiosity demonstrated by thousands of

Christians, Jews, Muslims, Buddhists, and Hindus all over the world. None of them believe God is dead.

- Trying to comprehend the fact that you've been through Mexico City, Guatemala City, San Salvador, Panama City, Lima, Santiago, Buenos Aries, Sao Paulo, Rio de Janeiro, Casablanca, Madrid, Paris, Munich, Belgrade, Venice, Saloniki, Istanbul, Tehran, Kabul, Lahore, New Delhi, Bombay, Tokyo. And who do you know who has driven the ALCAN Highway south from Anchorage?

- Listening to John Denver sing "Rocky Mountain High" on a car radio as you drive to Denver through a blaze of autumn Aspen gold in the most beautiful mountains in the world. How can you make this statement? Because you've crossed the Andes, the Alps and traveled the Khyber Pass within recent weeks . . .

- The sounds of Herat, Afghanistan, where aristocratic horses clip-clopped through town pulling beautifully varnished hansoms, their bells ringing like those of a Minnesota sleigh, counterpointing the eerie and monotonous sundown chant of the Muslims.

- The smells of Mexican spices; pines of the Alps; black fumes from poor gasoline; freshly threshed wheat in Turkey—often thrown onto the road for "tire threshing"; your first taste of unleavened bread right from the stone oven in the Middle East; smoke from a lone Bacumba [voodoo] candle burning at sundown at Copacabana beach in Rio; freshy fallen snow in the Andes and Rockies.

- The tastes of Mexican tortillas, enchiladas, tacos—the cheaper and dirtier the place, the better they were; the incredibly hot and spicy chicken Tandori of India, enjoyed in a primitive restaurant in New Delhi where you watched a perspiring baker sit before a stone pit oven on the floor; the refreshing taste of ice cold, pasteurized milk from

one of hundreds of roadside dairy bars on a scorching hot
day in India; your first American ham and eggs breakfast
at 3 a.m. in three months, in the Captain Hook hotel in
Anchorage . . .

Murphy served as a spokesperson for STP, traveling around the country in support of their book, *Car Care for Women.*

LandSpeed Productions Research Library / Paula Murphy Collection

Chapter 6

Finishing the Ride

"It was exciting. It was dangerous. It was fast. It was thrilling."
—Linda Vaughn on drag racing in the 1970s

As if spending one-hundred-plus days driving a Pontiac Sunbird around the planet through all conditions imaginable wasn't enough for one year, Murphy loaded the rest of her 1976 racing calendar with other notable moments.

With accommodations no longer available in her familiar Geneva-on-the-Lake spot, the team now worked out of entrepreneur Barry Setzer's shop just outside of Hickory, North Carolina. Setzer had been teamed earlier with driver Pat Foster, campaigning a successful Chevy Vega Funny Car in the early '70s.

When Murphy and Bynum parked the Funny Car for good, "Fat Jack" moved on and went to work for Foster.

"When he and Paula quit running her Funny Car, I grabbed him to go on the road with the Setzer car," Foster told DragList.com. "To a man, everyone told me I was nuts. Jack, a tuner? Crew chief? Not a chance . . . Wrong! Jack and I, with very little other help, took the car on tour and soon let the match-race junkies know there was definitely a new sheriff in town."

In the spring, at the age of forty-eight, Murphy returned to Alabama International Motor Speedway in Talladega with backing again from Granatelli and STP, intent to better her women's closed-course record she had set in 1971 in Fred Lorenzen's ride. Getting a little coaching prior to the run from NASCAR Hall of Famer and seven-time NASCAR Cup Series champion Richard Petty, a fellow STP-sponsored driver, didn't hurt.

"That's a tough combination," Murphy told the *Charlotte Observer*'s Tom Higgins. "I'm confident I can set a record over a closed course that will stand for some time."

Stock Car Racing magazine's Richard Benyo set the scene:

The run was scheduled at noon, an hour before the scheduled start of the ARCA 200 stock car race. As a result, there were approximately 10,000 fans in the stands to watch the attempt. The area had been heavily rained on the day before, and the sky was still overcast, but the track racing surface was dry. There was a pool of water at the entrance to pit road.

After a few warm-up laps, during which the engine sounded rough and seemed to be missing, Paula Murphy brought the car back in for some adjustments. Then it was back on to the track for the record attempt.

Driving Petty's STP Dodge that powered The King to the 1974 Winston Cup Championship, Murphy pushed the Chrysler

426-cubic-inch Hemi to a new mark of 172.344 miles per hour. Scoring the record on her first of several attempts, always the racer, Murphy was looking for more in the rebuilt car prepared by Richard Petty Engineering.

Murphy with the familiar STP No. 43 of NASCAR legend Richard Petty, a ride she took to a record speed of 172.336 mph in 1976, topping her own women's closed-course mark. *NASCAR Archives & Research Center*

The speed, which earned a quick kiss from Petty himself, would have qualified Murphy for that year's Talladega 500.

"I would have liked to have gone 175," she told reporters. "But, I'm just happy to be able to break the old record [171.499]. However, I guess my leg was shaking too bad for me to push the pedal down. Seriously, I didn't want to take any risks. I haven't been in this kind of car in five years."

Not bad for a hot rod driven the day before by—comedian Jerry Lewis? Lewis, in town for about an hour to gather footage for his annual twenty-four-hour *MDA Labor Day Telethon* for Muscular Dystrophy, chauffeured Petty around the Talladega community and town square as part of a ceremony making both Lewis and Petty honorary citizens of the city.

With Janet Guthrie in town to attempt to qualify for the Winston Cup Series race, Murphy's opinions on women not being physically equipped to compete in the long-distance NASCAR and USAC events again made headlines.

"They're just not going to be successful," Murphy told the *Ft. Lauderdale News* just days after the effort. "I've driven every kind of car there is, and I think I know what I am talking about.

"I'm still stiff and sore [from driving the Petty car]," she added. "You really have to hang onto the wheel. I couldn't have ridden 500 miles, let alone driven 500 miles."

In an article for *Daily Press* in Newport News, Virginia, Murphy clarified that it wasn't due in any part to a woman's abilities. "It's not a mental thing," Murphy said. "We have the courage and the capacity to do it. It's the physical difficulty of driving the car. A Grand National car weighs 4,000 pounds." Of note, NASCAR did not have power steering until 1981, when it was introduced by driver Geoff Bodine.

While qualifying for the Firecracker 400 at Talladega just a few months later, Guthrie fell just short of Murphy's run with a lap at 172.120 mph. She did, however, go on to qualify and compete in

Murphy showing off the record run numbers with Richard
Petty (left) and Bill France Jr. (right), who had succeeded his
father as NASCAR president just a few years earlier. *LandSpeed
Productions Research Library / Paula Murphy Collection*

five NASCAR events in 1976, including the grueling World 600,
where she finished fifteenth. Failing to qualify for the Indianapolis
500 in 1976, Guthrie would qualify and race in the next three Indy
500s from 1977 to 1979, becoming the first woman to race in both
the Daytona 500 and Indianapolis 500.

Back to Dragging

Back in the straight-line world, Murphy stepped down from the power and speed of the Funny Car in favor of a highly modified and factory-supported Datsun 1200 Coupe designed and built by Pete Brock. Racing in the NHRA B-Modified Compact Class, Murphy continued competing under the "Miss STP" moniker, but without Bynum or, in most cases, her son, Danny, who had given up on any hope of inheriting the Funny Car ride a few summers before and moved on to other interests.

"I had to get back into dragging," Murphy told United Press International. "In dragging, racing is the big challenge. It's an 'ego trip.' When you're well known, it makes you feel kind of good."

Murphy also raced a FWD/Stock Honda Civic before eventually retiring. According to an article in *Super Stock & Drag Illustrated*, Murphy was introduced to Honda representatives at Daytona, where she was participating in the Union/Pure Oil Performance Trials.

"They built me a car," Murphy explained in the article. "I'd go to tech inspection and no one knew where to begin looking at it if it won, which I did a couple of times. We had a ball with that car and never had any breakage until the end of the year when we went up to Seattle for an NHRA event and the trans went away. So, we parked the car and never ran that one again."

Relating another Honda story for the magazine, Murphy shared some of the fun around driving one of the first front-wheel-drive drag cars. "When I had the Honda, Goodyear gave me some road race tires," Murphy said. "We put those little fat slicks on the front, and I was waiting to make a run at the Winternationals at Pomona. There was no lettering on the car or anything, and no one knew who I was. This guy came up to me and said, 'Hey lady, don't you think you ought to put the slicks on the back?' I said, 'No, why?' And he said, 'Because that's where they're supposed to go.' I replied, 'Well, you idiot, if you'd look, you'd see that it's front-wheel drive.'"

"I had a lot of fun in those little cars," said Murphy, who officially announced her retirement from drag racing in April 1977. "STP was still involved, and I toured with both of them."

Extending her racing career by a few years in the small-car category, Murphy also went back to work full-time, signing on as a racing consultant with Centerline Tool Co., maker of racing and high-performance aluminum wheels. She ended up with nearly the entire sales promotion department under her direction, while also continuing her work as a traveling spokesperson for everything from car shows to child car seat safety.

In 1978, Murphy toured the country for STP, headlining clinics and promoting their book, *Car Care for Women*, stressing the importance of women being able to do basic car maintenance. Murphy was quoted in *Baltimore Sun*, saying, "Personally, I simply don't like to do tune-ups. But I do think every woman should know how."

Bynum Returns

Nearly twenty years later, the "team" reunited when Bynum surprised Danny, then working as a maintenance supervisor for Anheuser-Busch, with a visit.

"It was around nineteen ninety-four or ninety-five and it was about nine o'clock at night," Danny recalled. "The guard shack calls and says, 'There's a truck driver out here who says he has a truckload of hydraulic fittings for you.' I did order stuff like that and we were right in the middle of an overhaul on the line and we had ordered a lot of parts. I didn't usually order them, but we had a guy who did, and it was not impossible that a truckload of things might show up at odd hours.

"In comes the truck and out jumps this guy," Danny added. "He has a big beard, and his hair is long, and he's wearing the blue-striped bib overalls like train engineers used to wear; they were cut off to make them into shorts . . . he was wearing Doc Marten boots. I didn't even recognize him.

"I forget what he said, but I knew right then and there, 'Fat Jack' had come back from obscurity," Danny continued.

Bynum was struggling with health issues, and Paula was there to help. "They had been gasoline and matches at times, but she understood his value and they had a mutual respect," Danny said.

Bynum and Murphy married briefly, in part to allow Bynum to get an expensive medical procedure. After recovering from the surgery, the marriage eventually was annulled, and everyone went their separate ways again.

Murphy, while never romantically attached to Bynum, felt an obligation to help her former mechanic and friend after all their years together on the road. "Jack had done a lot for me," Murphy said.

"About six months to a year later, we found out that Jack had passed away," Danny said.

It was reported that he died "suddenly but peacefully at his home in Austin, Texas," on March 13, 1999, at the age of sixty-one. The obituary was short and to the point, with no mention of his adventures in drag racing, concluding with "No services were planned."

Hall of Fame

In 1992, Murphy began receiving recognition for her long list of motorsports accomplishments, first being inducted into the International Drag Racing Hall of Fame in 1992.

"I got really, really lucky," she said for an article in *National Dragster*. "I don't think many people have gotten the opportunity to do some of the things that I did. I don't look at myself as anything special; it was just the time for a woman to try to drive a Funny Car, and I felt rather proud that I was the one."

In 2004, Murphy served as Grand Marshal of the California Hot Rod Reunion. Held annually at Famoso Dragstrip in Bakersfield, California, the reunion brings together drag racers from throughout the sport's history, with an event newsletter noting, "There aren't many events where almost everyone asks each other for autographs and to have pictures taken."

In 2016, Murphy and Don Schumacher returned to the UK to celebrate their 1973 three-race appearance at Santa Pod Raceway and the HMS Daedalus air base. The British Drag Racing Hall of Fame brought the pair together at its annual Gala Awards Dinner. The next year, Murphy was named to the West Coast Sports Hall of Fame and inducted into the prestigious Motorsports Hall of Fame of America as a drag racer. Fellow inductees included five-time Rolex 24 champion Scott Pruett; sprint car giant Steve Kinser; three-time DAYTONA 200 motorcycle champion Dick Klamfoth; two-time NASCAR Cup Series champion Terry Labonte; Herb Thomas, another two-time NASCAR Cup Series titlist; and multifaceted legend Brock Yates. Murphy was inducted by longtime friend and fellow match-race sensation, "TV Tommy" Ivo.

Longtime friend and fellow racer "TV Tommy" Ivo inducted Murphy into the Motorsports Hall of Fame of America in 2017. *LandSpeed Productions Research Library / Paula Murphy Collection*

While attending the event in Daytona, Murphy had to excuse herself and was taken to a nearby hospital with a bout of diverticulitis. Her grandchildren, Kevin and Christina, stayed to represent her, with Christina reading Paula's speech—a racer's speech indeed:

To date, there are only six women who have been inducted into the Motorsports Hall of Fame—Jacqueline Cochran, Betty Cook, Amelia Earhart, Shirley Muldowney, Betty Skelton, and now me. This, to me, is like winning an Oscar, Emmy, and Grammy all rolled into one. Many thanks for selecting me for this honor.

There were many wonderful people who provided and encouraged me in my drag racing career.

To name a few:

Don Garlits, who signed my very first fuel license. Don is a legend in our sport, an innovator, and an inspiration to all.

Second on my list is Andy Granatelli, former President of STP, and my major sponsor. Without Andy and STP, I never would have had the thrill of driving a Funny Car, co-setting 360 USAC records at Bonneville, driving coast to coast across the US for a transcontinental speed record, twice setting the women's land speed record and NASCAR closed course—or becoming the first woman allowed on the Indianapolis Motor Speedway in a race car.

Next, is my father [Paul] and son, Danny, who put up with a daughter and mother doing crazy things and running all over the world. My son has never forgiven me for not letting him drive my Funny Car.

I also owe a huge debt to Jack Bynum, my friend and mechanic.

Also, Goodyear and Valvoline, who furnished me all the tires and oil I could burn out and burn up. As a side point, when our two-car Bicentennial Global Record Run team drove around the world for Pontiac and National Rental Car, I selected Goodyears for my car and Johnnie Parson's went with Firestone. Parsons had four tire failures. I had none.

All in all, the years I spent in racing were very good to me, despite my crash in a rocket car at Scars Point. I made many wonderful friends, and of course it was perfect earning my living doing something I really loved.

Thank you again for this great honor, it will be moment in time that I will remember and cherish forever.

Murphy's career started with the purchase of a little red MG and a tagalong visit with friends to California car club races. It twisted and turned through the Bonneville salt, the Indy bricks, the Talladega high banks, the Baja desert, quarter miles of concrete and asphalt from California to England, and roads that weren't even roads all around the world.

Career Accomplishments

Her list of accomplishments include but are not limited to:

- Successful SCCA sports car racer in the 1950s
- Multi-year competitor in the Mobil Transcontinental Economy Run beginning in 1961
- Drove a Studebaker Avanti from Los Angeles to New York for a coast-to-coast speed record of 49 hours and 37 minutes in 1963
- Achieved an average speed of 161.29 mph through the "flying mile" at Bonneville in a Studebaker, setting the women's land-speed record of 172 mph with an internal combustion engine; Murphy was part of a crew sponsored by Studebaker that set 300-plus speed records at Bonneville during one week in October 1963

- First woman to drive at speed at Indianapolis Motor Speedway in 1963
- Became the "Fastest Woman on Wheels," piloting Walt Arfons's jet-powered Avenger to a two-way average speed of 226.37 mph in 1964
- First woman licensed in the NHRA Funny Car division; competed successfully for nearly a decade in match races around the country
- Competed in multiple off-road endurance races, including the Baja 1000, Baja 500, and Mint 400

Murphy sits in the Chevy Camaro pace car for the 2009 Indianapolis 500. At the age of eighty-one, more than forty years after becoming the first woman to drive the historic track, she made four laps around Indy in the 2010 Camaro with three-time Indy 500 champion Johnny Rutherford riding shotgun and Murphy's pal, "LandSpeed" Louise Noeth in the back seat. She topped out at around 150 mph. *LandSpeed Productions Research Library / Paula Murphy Collection*

- Voted one of four groundbreaking women athletes by the Associated Press in 1972
- Won more individual events than any other driver in the 1968 Union/Pure Oil Performance Trials
- Piloted the ill-fated Pollution Packer rocket car through the Bonneville quarter mile in 6.2 seconds in 1972; also hit a speed of 258 mph at the NHRA Winternationals in the same car in 1973
- Drove around the world in a record 104 days as part of the US Bicentennial Global Record Run in 1976; the effort, supported by National Car Rental and Pontiac, took Murphy and 1950 Indianapolis 500 winner Johnnie Parsons across five continents and twenty-nine countries
- Ran twice at what is now Talladega Superspeedway, both times setting women's national closed-course records; the second run in 1976 was at 172.344 mph in a car prepared by Richard Petty Engineering

Ironically, after nearly dying on a hill at Sears Point when the rocket car she was piloting went out of control, Murphy spent the lion's share of her post-racing career as a buyer for Rocketdyne, a rocket engine design and production company headquartered near Los Angeles. Looking back on it all in her mid nineties, Murphy remains ready to race and shares her secret to a long life.

Her nearly daily routine up until breaking her leg in the spring of 2023—a single beer with nuts or pretzels at three in the afternoon; at seven or eight, a half glass of wine with ice and sparkling water, and then at nine or ten, a shot of peach vodka before going to bed.

Never one to brag about all her accomplishments, her passion for driving still shines through. "I would go, I would still go, but nothing like what I drove previously," Murphy said with more than a hint of seriousness and an obvious yearning for a little speed in

Murphy didn't spend a lot of time looking back on her life, instead choosing to be firmly on the gas and always moving forward. *LandSpeed Productions Research Library / Paula Murphy Collection*

her life. "A stock car of some sort would be fun to set a land-speed record, maybe in a lower-class car."

At a recent event to honor her career at the Petersen Automotive Museum in Los Angeles, Murphy made her selection clear: "A Porsche."

At the event, "LandSpeed" Louise Noeth paid the ultimate tribute: "As far as I am concerned, Paula Murphy, she is the pioneer that allowed other women to put on helmets all over the world because she blazed the trail in so many different aspects in motorsports," Noeth said for Santa Barbara's News Channel 3. "I take my helmet off to Paula because she helped other women put them on."

Anyone want to bet against her?

Bibliography

"Adele Von Ohl Parker." *Encyclopedia of Cleveland History.*
    Case Western Reserve University. https://case.edu/ech/
    articles/p/parker-adele-von-ohl.

Alsop, Kay. "Her Driving Ambition." *The Province*, September 16,
    1976.

Andy Granatelli Archives. Archives Center, Smithsonian
    National Museum of American History. Kenneth E. Behring
    Center.

Benyo, Richard. "Paula Murphy." *Stock Car Racing*, September 1,
    1976.

"Bicentennial Global Record Run Begins." *USAC News*, July 8,
    1976.

Burgess, Phil. "Female Funny Car Pioneer Paula Murphy."
    National Dragster, March 11, 2016.

"Charlotte 1974: The Good, The Bad and The Ugly."
    Competition Plus, September 1, 2008. https://www.
    competitionplus.com/drag-racing/news/7635-encore-charlotte-
    1974-the-good-the-bad-the-ugly#.

Chase, Don. "Paula Teaches 'Em a Thing or Two."
    Las Vegas Sun, February 5, 1973.

"Drivers Ready to Embark on Bicentennial Journey."
    Palm Beach Post, July 4, 1976.

"Fastest Woman on Wheels." *Auto Topics*, April 1, 1965.

Finston, Mark. "Global Spin Promises Ride on the Wild Side." *New Jersey Star-Ledger*, June 24, 1976.

Foster, Pat. "Drag Racing List—Fat Jack Bynum." DragList.com, March 27, 2004. https://www.draglist.com/artman2/publish/daily_stories/Fat_Jack_Bynum_449.shtml.

"Funny Cars All-Star Cast at Assumption." *The Decatur Daily Review*, June 12, 1971.

Geiger, Kay B. "It Beats Desk Work." *The Decatur Daily Review*, June 15, 1971.

"Go Round the World by Car." *Ville Platte Gazette*, November 18, 1976.

"Good to Be American." *The Moline Dispatch*, October 24, 1976.

Houlgate, Deke. "John Cannon Bypasses Can-Am Series." *Progress Bulletin*, April 10, 1969.

———. "Paula Murphy." *Stock Car Racing*, September 1, 1976.

Hower, George. "Meet Paula Murphy—World's Fastest Woman." *The Press Democrat*, September 23, 1973.

Hyland, Dick. "Michelmore Wins." *Los Angeles Times*.

Ireland, Charles. "Ken Miles Pilots Ferrari to Victory." *Santa Barbara News-Press*, May 28, 1962.

Kelly, Steve. "Funny Girl." *Hot Rod*, March 1, 1970.

Kirk, Andy. "The Amazing Career of Paula Murphy." STP-UK.com. https://www.studebaker-info.org/Bonneville/PaulaMurphy2/pm2.html.

"Land Speed Record for Women Broken." *New York Times*, November 13, 1964.

Laurence, Bee. "Paula Murphy: Riding a Rocket Car into Orbit." *Napa Valley Register*, September 27, 1973.

Lee, Tom. "Around the World in 102 Days." *Omaha World Herald*, February 6, 1977.

Littlefield, Larry. "No Rockets for the Speedy Lady." *Times-Advocate*, November 30, 1975.

Lohnes, Brian. "Vintage Drag Video: Legendary American Racers Running at Santa Pod Raceway in England." Bangshift.com, January 12, 2010.

Martin, Gordon. "This Lady's in a Hurry." *San Francisco Chronicle*, February 11, 1970.

McFarland, Jim. "The Female and the Fueler." *Hot Rod*, March 1, 1967.

McKee, Sandra. "Paula Murphy Helps to Keep Women's Cars on the Go." *The Baltimore Sun*, October 27, 1978.

Murphy, Paula. "My Ride at Talladega." *Stock Car Racing*, December 1, 1971.

Nelson, Karen. "Personality Profile: Paula Murphy." *Drag Racing*, July 1, 1967.

Noeth, Louise. *Images of Modern America: Bonneville's Women of Land Speed Racing*. Charleston, SC: Arcadia Publishing, 2021.

Olsen, Jack. "Duel on the Salt." *Sports Illustrated*, December 6, 1965.

———. "My Brother, My Enemy in Speedland." *Sports Illustrated*, November 29, 1965.

Ottenheimer, Miles. "Queen of the Snowmobiles." *The San Francisco Examiner*, March 1, 1970.

Ottum, Bob. "Duel with Death on the Salt." *Sports Illustrated*, November 28, 1966.

Parker, Eddi. "Racing 'Bug' Really Bites, Paula Finds." *Akron Beacon-Journal*, July 30, 1964.

Parsons, Johnnie. *Johnnie Parsons— Never Look Back*. Marshall, IN: Witness Productions, 2005.

"Paula Murphy—World's Fastest Woman Driver." *The Montgomery Advertiser*, November 22, 1973.

Presley, Merikaye. "It's Around the World in 60 Days— Via Auto." *Times-Picayune*, July 8, 1976.

Racing Sports Cars (RSC) Archives.

Rayner, Polly. "Life a Drag—and She Loves It." *The Morning Call*, January 22, 1975.

Rickman, Eric. "Powder Puff Mustang." *Hot Rod*. April 1, 1967.

Sanders, Clare. "Drag Racing Story of the Day—Fat Jack's Charm School." DragList.com. https://www.draglist.com/stories/SOD%20Apr%202000/SOD-042900.htm.

"Saugus Main Event Win for Governale." *Van Nuys News*, August 21, 1962.

Scagnetti, Jack. "Ms. PPP's Gasser." *Performance Cars*, February 1, 1973.

Shulte, Ellen. "Gal Race Driver: It's a Drag Sometimes." *Los Angeles Times*, January 19, 1968.

Stephan, Art. "Two Women Drivers in Long Test Drive." *Long Beach Press-Telegram*, September 11, 1963.

Strawbridge, Connie. "Paula Murphy: Confessions of the First Female Fuel Racer." *Super Stock & Drag Illustrated*, May 1, 1989.

Sweat, Earl. "Murphy Motors Through." *Mobile Press Register*, October 17, 1976.

Thomas, Bob. "Cross Country 'Dash' No Strain for 2 Gals, Guy." *Los Angeles Times*, September 8, 1963.

———. "Krause Pilots Maserati to Victory at Pomona." *Los Angeles Times*, January 9, 1961.

———. "Krause Starts Last, Drives 'Crippled' Car to Victory." *Los Angeles Times*, August 20, 1962.

Thomas, Roy. "Murphy Serious About Today's Run." *The Montgomery Advertiser*, April 20, 1971.

Tinsley, Jeff. "Paula Murphy's STP Duster." *Super Stock & Drag Illustrated*, November 1, 1972.

Walordy, Alex. "Paula Murphy: The Fastest Lady Driver in the World." *Super Stock & Drag Illustrated*, December 1, 1971.

What's My Line? YouTube/CBS.

White, Karen. "Paula Murphy: She's a Lady and the Fastest Woman on Wheels." *Santa Maria Times*, January 30, 1973.

Wilkens, Emily. "Plan Vacation." *The Jersey Journal*, January 14, 1977.

"Woman Driver—EGAD!—To Enter Sports Car Meet."
Van Nuys News, July 15, 1962.

Young, Ken. "Mrs. Murphy's Mauler." *Speed and Supercar,*
December 1, 1971.

Author Interviews

Dan ("Danny") Murphy
Danny Thompson
Darrell Gwynn
Dave Densmore
Della Wood
Don Schumacher
Don "The Snake" Prudhomme
Ed McLean
George Calloway
H. A. "Humpy" Wheeler
"LandSpeed" Louise Noeth
Linda Vaughn
Lynda McCourry
Paula Murphy
Shirley Muldowney
Steve Gibbs
Tim Grose
"TV Tommy" Ivo

Index

Adam-Mitchell Special 1600, 30, 36
Aguilar Inzunza, Manuel, 112
Alabama International Motor
    Speedway (Talladega
    Superspeedway), 81–82, 83–85,
    128–31, 139
Alfa Romeo, 31
Allison, Bobby, 109
American Hot Rod Association
    (AHRA), 60, 68
Anderson, Bonnie, 56
Anderson, Dave, 88, 89, 94, 96, 100
The Anniston Star (newspaper), 61
Arfons, Art, 16, 17–19, 88, 95, 96
Arfons, Walt, xv–xvi, xvii–xxi, 15, 20
Associated Press (AP), 6
Atco Dragway, New Jersey, 66, 74
Auto Racing Magazine, 42
Auto Topics, 16
Avanti, 2, 8, 38, 40
Avenger, xvii, xx, 3–7

Baja 500, California, 78
Baker, Sunnie, 36
Baltimore Sun, 133
Banks, Henry, 108
Barracuda (Plymouth), 60, 69
Barry, Mike, 77
"Battle of the Sexes" tennis
    tournament, 90–91
Beadle, Raymond, 91
Beaumont, Marie-Claude, 102

Below, Lucy, 56
Benyo, Richard, 128
Beswick, Arnie "The Farmer," 79
Bloemker, Al, 42
Bonneville Salt Flats, Utah
    challenges of, 1, 10
    description of, 11
    driving conditions of, 10, 15
    features of, 8
    land speed record at, xvi–xxi
    Paula Murphy at, xv, xvi
    photo of, xvii, xx, 87, 94, 96
    policies of, 15–16
    Pollution Packer rocket car at, 87–90
    speed records at, 2
Breedlove, Craig, 16, 20, 88, 96
Breedlove, Lee, 16, 20
British Drag Racing Hall of Fame, 135
Brock, Pete, 132
Brodie, John, 74
Brown, Jean, 57
Buffalo Bill's Wild West show, 27
Burkett, Bunny, 56
Burkhardt, "Big Mike," 80
Burlingame, Byers A., 17
Bynum, Jack "Fat Jack"
    acclaim for, 136
    in car culture, 70
    characteristics of, 63, 81
    death of, 134
    personal relationship of, 72, 134
    responsibilities of, 67, 68

return of, 133–34
work of, 46, 48–49, 50, 80–81, 128

Cagle, Clarence, 42
California Hot Rod Reunion, 134–35
Calloway, George, 10
Calvin, Jean, 30, 33, 35
Car Care for Women, 133
Carroll, Bill, 37, 40
Carter, Nelson, 64
Cass, Mama, 74
The Castaway, 65–66
catboating, 26
Centerline Tool Co., 133
Century Run, Florida, 82
Charlotte Motor Speedway, North
    Carolina, 86–87, 100
Charlotte Observer, 128
Citroën ID19, 33–34
Clark, Jim, 20
Cochran, Jacqueline, 136
Community Chest (United Way), 28
Competition Plus, 100
Cook, Betty, 136
Cox, Carol, 56
Cox, Tom, 78
Cyclops jet car, 16, 17–18

Daily Press, 130
Daly, John, 2
Daniel, Tom, 86
Datsun 1200 Coupe, 132
Davidson, Donald, 109, 118, 123
Davis, Dorothy, 56
Daytona 500, 131
Daytona Beach News-Journal, 111
Daytona International Speedway,
    Florida, 109, 110–11
The Decatur Daily Review, 78
Deist, Jim, 10
Densmore, Dave, 53
Dodge Charger Super Chief, 64
drag racing. *See also* Funny Car class;
    specific drivers and tracks
    appeal of, 50

fatalities from, 55, 100–101
features of, 51
licensing in, 52–53
Miss Universe of Drag Racing, 57
outlaw tracks of, 54–55
Paula Murphy's return to, 132–33
powder puff classes in, 57
process of, 50–51
schedule of, 71
women in, 51–52, 54, 56
Drag Racing magazine, 36–37, 47, 50–51
Dredge, Bill, 6, 37, 41, 82
Driving Line, 109
Drysdale, Don, 74
Durachrome Bug, 65
Duster (Plymouth), 86

Earhart, Amelia, 136
Eckerman, Bernice, 56
Economaki, Chris, 111
Elliott, Janet, 74
English, John E., 31
Epton, Joe, 84
Evans, Vince "Pea Soup," 79

Famoso Dragstrip, California, 134–35
"Fat Jack's Charm School," 61–64, 65
Ferrari, Testa Rossa, 32
Filline, Tom, 40
Firecracker 400, 130–31
Firestone, 16, 18, 20
Fisher, Dorothy, 56
Floyd Clymer's Auto Topics magazine,
    xix, xvii
Follmer, George, 60
Foss-Jackson, Mary Ann, 56
Foster, Pat, 49, 127, 128
Fox, Tony, 87, 88, 90, 94, 96
Foyt, A. J., 109
France, Bill, 85
France, Bill, Jr., 131
Ft. Lauderdale News, 130
Fullerton, Larry, 79
Funny Car class, 49–50, 51, 71, 77. *See also*
    drag racing; specific drivers and tracks

Gabelich, Gary, 88, 96
Gallagher, Patrick, 66–67
Garlits, Don "Big Daddy," 52, 57, 70, 91, 136
Garner, James, 79
Gatornationals (NHRA), 89
Gennuso, Rose Marie, 57
Gibbs, Steve, 55, 100–101
Giulietta Spider, 31
Goins, Nellie, 56
Goins, Otis, 56
Goldsmith, Paul, 82
Goodyear, 16, 18, 20, 132
Graham, Athol, 8, 9
Granatelli, Andy
  influence of, 41
  leadership of, xvi, 1, 2, 6, 11–12, 21, 51, 56, 81, 136
  photo of, 17
  quote of, 42
  split of, 85
  success of, 9
Granatelli, Joe, 1, 9
Granatelli, Vince, 1, 9
Gran Turismo Hawk, 2
"The Great American Off-Road Race," 74
Great Lakes Dragway, Wisconsin, 72, 88
Green Valley Raceway, Texas, 60
Grose, Tom, 62, 64, 66–67
Gunter, Warren, 65
Gustin, Roger, 96
Guthrie, Janet, 109, 130–31
Gwynn, Darrell, 91

Hamilton, Barbara, 55, 56
Hampshire, Ronnie, 51
Hardy, Don, 60, 69
Haywards, Owen, 92
Hemmings Motor News, 17–18
Hendron, Bettie, 57
Henson, Carol, 57
Hickey, Vic, 86
Higgins, Tom, 128

Hill, Nobby, 92
Honda Civic, 132
Hoover, Tom, 79–80, 86
horse riding/shows, 26–28
Hot Rod magazine, xviii, 2, 42, 51–52, 53
Houlgate, Deke, 42, 79
Houndog 7 car, 92
Huff, Frank, 64, 65
Hulman, Tony, 42
Huszar, Frank, 73

Indianapolis 500, 43–45, 131, 138
Inter-Lake Yachting Association Regatta, 25–26
International Hot Rod Association (IHRA), 68, 86–87, 100
Iron Duke (Pontiac), 109
Ivo, Tommy, 64, 70–71, 72, 135

James, Joe W., 108
Jenkins, Ab, 8
jet cars, 8, 9, 12, 18–19. *See also specific drivers and cars*
Jones, Deacon, 74
Jones, Parnelli, 74

Kalitta, Connie, 57, 68–69
Keller, Dick, 88
Kennedy, John F., 14
Kile, Carol, 57
King, Billie Jean, 90–91
Kings Castle Grand Prix, Nevada, 74
Kinser, Steve, 135
Klamfoth, Dick, 135
Knievel, Evel, 74
Kuchenbecker Muhlhauser, Libbie Augusta, 24, 29–30

Labonte, Terry, 135
Lake Bonneville, 8
Landy, Dick, 48
Lardnan, Raul Maliay, 123
Laurence, Bee, 96–97
Lee, Tom, 109, 122–25, 123

Leong, Roland, 81
Lewis, Jerry, 130
Lieberman, "Jungle Jim," 52, 86
Life Magazine, 6, 19, 20
Lions Drag Strip, Wilmington,
    California, 49
Long Beach Press-Telegram, 38
Lorenzen, Fred, 78, 81–82, 85, 128
Los Angeles and Orange County
    Oldsmobile Dealers Association, 48
Los Angeles Times, 32, 33, 40, 60
Louis, Joe, 74
Lynch, Rich, 55

Maas, Butch, 79
MacAfee, Jack, 31
Mahaffey, Wayne, 86
Marvin, Lee, 74
McCourry, Lynda, 64
McCourry, Tom, 64
McDonald, Dave, 45
McEwen, Tom "The Mongoose," 52
McLean, Ed, 109
Mellot, Fan, 57
Mendenhall, Jack, 78, 86
Michaelson, Ky "Rocketman," 87, 92–93
Mignone, Steve, 109, 123
Miles, Ken, 31
Miller, Sammy, 91
Mint 400, 74, 78, 79, 86
Miss Universe of Drag Racing, 57
Mobilgas Economy Run, 33, 38–39
Mobil Mileage Rally, 33–37
Modern Rod magazine, xvi, xix, 13
Monte Carlo Grand Prix, 102–5
Mormon Meteor, 8
The Morning Call, 96, 99
Motion Raceway, Illinois, 79–80
Motorsports Hall of Fame of America,
    135
MotorTrend magazine, 23
Mueller, John, 109, 123
Muhlhauser, Paul, 24–25, 28, 29–30, 136
Muldowney, Shirley, 52, 55, 57, 68–70,
    136

Murphy, Dan, 28, 29
Murphy, Danny
    acclaim for, 136
    activities of, 65–66
    birth of, 28
    Jack Bynum and, 72–74, 133–34
    photo of, 53
    quote of, 91–92
    viewpoint of, 50
    work of, 61, 67–68, 80–81
Murphy, Paula
    acclaim for, 52, 64–65, 72, 81, 141
    career accomplishments of, 137–39
    car of, 28–29
    childhood of, 24–25
    coast-to-coast racing by, 37–40
    crash of, 97–100
    criticism of, 13
    daily routine of, 139
    divorce of, 29
    dream of, 96
    earnings of, xvi, 46, 68
    education of, 28
    as equestrian, 26–28
    family of, 24
    Hall of Fame and, 134–41
    home of, 24, 61–63
    illness of, 136
    injuries of, 37, 72, 97–98, 99
    licensing of, 52–53, 54, 55–56
    marriage of, 28, 29, 134
    as mother, 73
    passion of, 139–41
    photo of, xvii, xx, xxii, 9, 17, 19, 21,
        22, 25, 26, 29, 34, 35, 36, 38, 41,
        43, 44, 45, 46, 53, 58, 62, 71, 73,
        76, 83, 85, 87, 90, 93, 95, 96, 99,
        106, 110, 114, 116, 117, 121, 126,
        129, 131, 135, 138, 140
    physical characteristics of, xv, xvii, 3
    popularity of, 11
    sailing and, 24–26
    "Speed Kings" trading card of, 12
    speed skating by, 23–24
    statistics of, 33–34

success of, 11
versatility of, 78
work of, 28, 133

Nancy, Tony, 91
Napa Valley Register, 96–97
NASCAR, 128–31
National Car Rental, 107–8, 109
National Dragster magazine, 61, 134
National Hot Rod Association (NHRA)
Gatornationals of, 89
licensing in, 53, 54, 56
Pacific Division of, 48
Springnationals of, 90
Stock Eliminator of, 48
women in, 54
Nelson, Cal, 51
Nelson, Karen, 47
Newark Star-Ledger, 108
New Jersey State Drag Racing
Championship, 74
New Orleans *Times-Picayune,* 108, 111
Nichels, Ray, 82
Nicholl, Jim, 65
Nieland, Barb, 1, 2, 9, 19, 37
Noeth, Louise, 14–16, 18, 138, 141
Novi (Studebaker), 41

Oglesby, Frank, 79
Olsen, Jack, xviii, 8, 18–19
Olympics of Drag Racing, 74
Omaha World Herald magazine, 122
Ottum, Bob, 41

Pacific Raceway Association (PRA), 32
Padilla & Spear, 108
Palamides, Romeo, 86, 91
Palm Beach Post, 111
Parker, Adele von Ohl, 27
Parker, Rob, 32
Parsons, Johnnie, 106, 108, 109, 111,
113, 115–16, 119, 120, 121, 137.
See also US Bicentennial Global
Record Run
Patrick, Scooter, 30

Paxson, John, 96
Pea Soup Ford pickup, 79
Pellegrini, Ron, 91–92
Penske, Roger, 31
Performance Cars magazine, 88–89
Petrali, Joe, xx–xxi, 38, 96
Petty, Richard, 109, 128–29, 131
Phelps, Bob, 91
Phelps, Roy, 91
Pink, Ed, 92
Plymouth Barracuda, 60, 69
Plymouth Duster, 86
Polak, Vasek, 31
Pollution Packer rocket car, 87–90,
92–97, 139
Pomona Road Race, California,
31–32
Pontiac Iron Duke, 109
Porsche RS-61, 43
Porsche Special, 33
Porsche Spyder, 34
Prince, Jack, 74
Prudhomme, Don "The Snake," 49–50
Pruett, Scott, 135

Raceway Hussy blog, 57
Ratliff, Franklin, 88
Rayner, Polly, 96
Reader's Digest, 19
Renault 5 Ladies' Monte Carlo Grand
Prix, Monte Carlo, 102–5
Reyes, Larry, 60
Riggs, Bobby, 90
Riverside International Raceway,
California, 60
Rocketdyne, 139
Root, Ron, 48
Rosburg, Bob, 74
Rose, Doug, 96
Rutherford, Johnny, 138

Sachs, Eddie, 40, 45
sailing, 24–26
Sanders, Clare, 61–62, 64
The San Francisco Examiner, 74, 118

Santa Barbara Memorial Day Race, California, 30
Santa Pod Raceway, England, 91–92, 93, 135
Santa Rosa Press Democrat, 93, 94
Saugus Stadium, 32
Scagnetti, Jack, 89
Schumacher, Don, 68, 86, 91, 92, 93, 135
Sears All-State Guardsman tires, 38
Sears Point Raceway, California, 92–98
Segrini, Al, 91
Setzer, Barry, 127
Shahan, Shirley, 57
Shelby Daytona, 16
Shutes, Betty, 32–33
Skelton, Betty, 16, 17–18, 136
Smith, Niamh Frances, 57
Smith, Tom "Smoker," 57
Snow, Gene, 91
Space Race, 13–14
Special Duster race car, 80–81
Speed and Supercar magazine, 45
"Speed Kings" trading card, 12
speed skating, 23–24
Spirit of America car, 16
Sports Illustrated, 8, 12–13, 18–19
Springnationals (NHRA), 90
Staley, Enoch, 109
Stephan, Art, 38
Stewart, Jackie, 104–05
Stock Car Racing magazine, 83–85, 102–04, 128
Stock Eliminator (NHRA), 48
STP
  overview of, 2
  publicity of, 11–12
  sponsorship of, xix, xxii, 18, 20, 45, 51, 70, 81, 82, 126, 133, 136
Stroppe, Bill, 79
Studebaker
  Avanti Sports Coupe, 38
  marketing of, 2, 4–6
  Novi, 41
  photo of, 9, 14

publicity of, 11–12, 14
sponsorship of, 20
Wagonaire, 40
Super Stock & Drag Illustrated, 55, 65, 80–81, 86, 93, 97, 132
Super Vega, 65

Talladega Superspeedway (Alabama International Motor Speedway), 81–82, 83–85, 128–31, 139
Tatroe, Bobby, xviii, 47
Taylor, Barbara, 111
Teal, Bryan, 62, 64
Tereshkova, Valentina, 14
Testa Rossa Ferrari, 32
Thacker, Tony, 30–31
Thomas, Herb, 135
Thompson, Danny, 10
Thompson, Mickey, 10, 86
Time-Mirror Grand Prix, California, 33
tires
  Firestone, 16, 18, 20
  Goodyear, 16, 18, 20, 132
  in Mobilgas Economy Run, 38, 40
  Sears All-State Guardsman, 38
  testing of, 40–41
  wars of, 18–19, 20
Titus, Jerry, 31
Tri-City Dragway, Michigan, 54

Union/Pure Oil Performance Trials, 58–59
United Press International (UPI), 6
United States Auto Club, timing slip of, 3–7
Unser, Bobby, 74
USAC News, 11, 115, 122
US Bicentennial Global Record Run
  Asia portion of, 115–17, 122–23, 124–25
  car types in, 109
  Central America portion of, 112–14
  challenges of, 120
  climate changes in, 111
  cost of, 109

delays in, 113
earnings in, 108
Europe portion of, 115–17, 122
logistics and statistics of, 118–19
Mexico portion of, 111–12, 123–24
Middle East portion of, 115–17, 122, 124
Northern Africa portion of, 115–17
overview of, 108, 122–25, 139
photo of, 110, 114, 116, 117, 119, 121, 123
South America portion of, 114–15, 122
United States portion of, 109–11, 118–19

Van Nuys News and Valley Green Sheet, 32
Vaughn, Linda, 81, 94–95, 127
Venturi, Ken, 74
Verne, Jules, 107
Ville Platte Gazette, 115, 118
von Ohl Parker, Adele, 27
Vukovich, Bill, 45

Wagonaire (Studebaker), 40
Walordy, Alex, 61, 63

Ward, Roger, 74
Watson, Ginger, 56
West Coast Sports Hall of Fame, 135
Weston, D. E., Jr., 2, 4
What's My Line?, 2
Wheeler, H. A. "Humpy," 1, 9, 10–11, 12, 15, 19
Wilson, Nancy, 57
Windeler, Ed, 109, 123
Windhorst, Barbara, 33
Women's Lib movement, 90–91
Women's Sports Car Club, 30
Wood, Carol, 57
Wood, Vicki, 82
Woods, Della, 54, 55, 79
World 600, 131
World Record Drag Race Championships (Charlotte Motor Speedway), 86–87

Yarborough, Cale, 109
Yates, Brock, 135
Yellow River Dragstrip, Georgia, 54–55
Young, Patty, 56
Yugoslavia, 108

About the Author

With more than thirty years in the sports media business, Erik Arneson is an award-winning author, having published racing biographies such as *Darrell Gwynn: At Full Throttle*, *John Force: The Straight Story of Drag Racing's 300-mph Superstar*, and *Mickey Thompson: Fast Life and Tragic Death of a Racing Legend*. His book on Thompson won a Bronze Medal at the International Automotive Media Awards (IAMA) in 2008, and Arneson was the NHRA Media Award winner in 1998 while writing for *USA Today*.

Made in United States
Orlando, FL
12 February 2024

43574140R00112